STRONG AND SOULFUL:
GRACED BY GRIEF

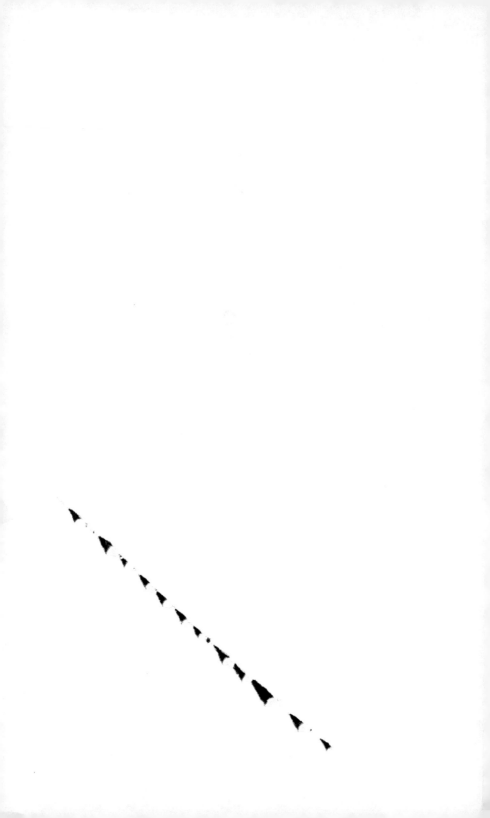

STRONG AND SOULFUL: GRACED BY GRIEF

DENISE OLSEN

MANUSCRIPTS
PRESS

STRONG AND SOULFUL: GRACED BY GRIEF

ISBN   979-8-88926-137-7   *Paperback*

979-8-88926-136-0   *Ebook*

979-8-88926-138-4   *Hardcover*

This book is dedicated to the love of my life, Jeff. You are the reason I am me. You loved me before I knew how to love myself, and even in death you have been my greatest teacher. It was an honor being your wife and the mother of your children. I know you are smiling down on me, elated that our story will make a difference in someone else's life. I promise to find you and love you in every lifetime. For now, I will live for both of us. Forever your girl.

Contents

INTRODUCTION 11

PART 1.   GRIEF   21

CHAPTER 1.   THE RECKONING   23

CHAPTER 2.   GRIEF DEFINED   33

CHAPTER 3.   WHAT IS A MEMORY,
             WHAT IS A NIGHTMARE?   41

CHAPTER 4.   THE ENERGY OF GRIEF   49

CHAPTER 5.   THE CLASH OF THE PAST AND PRESENT   59

CHAPTER 6.   SHADOWS AND LIGHT:
             FACTORS INFLUENCING GRIEF   75

CHAPTER 7.   PAIN IS A PRIVILEGE   89

CHAPTER 8.   COURAGE AND YOUR COMFORT ZONE   97

CHAPTER 9.   BREAKING CHAINS   109

CHAPTER 10. FROM TRAUMA TO TRANSFORMATION   117

PART 2.   G.R.A.C.E.   121

CHAPTER 11. G.R.A.C.E. DEFINED   123

CHAPTER 12. GRATITUDE   131

CHAPTER 13. CALMING THE STORM   137

CHAPTER 14. RADICAL ACKNOWLEDGMENT
           AND ACCEPTANCE   143

CHAPTER 15. THIS IS MY LIFE   149

CHAPTER 16. ACTION   153

CHAPTER 17. MOVEMENT AND INTENTION   161

CHAPTER 18. COMMUNITY   171

CHAPTER 19. NO ONE HEALS ALONE   177

CHAPTER 20. EMERGENT NARRATIVE   183

CHAPTER 21. YOU ARE THE MEANING MAKER   195

CHAPTER 22. SIGNS   201

CHAPTER 23. ONLY A THOUGHT AWAY   207

    CONCLUSION..211

    ACKNOWLEDGMENTS.............................. 219

    NOTES 225

"You will lose someone you can't live without, and your heart will be badly broken, and the bad news is that you never completely get over the loss of your beloved. But this is also the good news. They live forever in your broken heart that doesn't seal back up. And you come through. It's like having a broken leg that never heals perfectly—that still hurts when the weather gets cold, but you learn to dance with the limp."

—ANNE LAMOTT

Introduction

The end of September marks the onset of "local summer" for year-round residents of the Jersey Shore. With summer renters returning to their cities, the beaches and towns become less crowded, allowing one to truly appreciate the tranquility of the seaside towns along the southern New Jersey coast. I'm enjoying this stillness while walking my dogs along the usual path. We take the road on the side of our house down toward the inlet of water known as Glimmer Glass. We pass an empty field and a park along the way. The only sounds are crickets and the tap of my little pups' paws on the pavement. It is predawn, and the world is silently slumbering. The birds aren't yet chirping, and as I look over at the completely still water in the inlet, I can't help but think Glimmer Glass must be named for this time of day. The moon still hangs in the sky while the sun begins to announce its grand entrance with the most beautiful shades of orange and pink against the blue-black horizon. Most people are still tucked in their beds. It may be peaceful, but it wasn't always.

The glowing sky, the quiet calmness, and the serenity I am feeling as I walk my dogs immediately transport me back to the predawn hours of Wednesday, September 12, 2001. I am awake. I have been awake all night. Less than twenty-four hours ago, I watched as the North and South Towers of the World Trade Center collapsed, knowing my husband, Jeff, a NYC firefighter, was in there. I'm filled with a feeling I have never felt before—paralyzing fear.

Something has a vise grip around my center. Not just the center of my body but the center of my being. Breathing is painful. A lump in my throat won't go away. I am filled with this frenetic energy, a feeling of impending doom that I try to chase away with my thoughts, but like a child in a game of tag, it simply laughs and runs off in a different direction with me trying to keep up. It starts with the dull, aching pain in my heart and pulses to the outer edges of my fingers and toes. Over and over, every heartbeat echoes in my ears. My mind is creating scenarios—some unspeakable, some miraculous. None are true. Time is suspended, as if life has slammed on the brakes, and I am thrown from the car—floating, untethered, with the world flying by, bracing for impact. Yet I am sitting here on my front stoop, still and alone.

The early morning air is chilly, but I don't care. I can barely feel it. I can hardly feel anything. I have never been so numb. How can I feel numb and experience so much at the same time? This is all unchartered territory. Except for the explosion and collapse that is happening inside of me, it is quiet. The darkness feels like it will never end. This has been the longest night of my life. In hindsight, I understand the safety mechanism had already begun to kick in—the part of our biology that lessens the pain of that impact when we are about to crash.

The day begins to break... Slowly, the birds, one by one, are beginning to chirp. The chirping accumulates into a joyful chorus of birdsong, the antithesis to my inner experience of anguish. An old saying "time waits for no man" rushes through my mind. I can't believe the sun is rising so brilliantly, as if we hadn't just experienced the most devastating event of our lives.

Time, as it pertains to my current experience, seems frozen. My life appears to be in suspended animation. I feel as if my whole existence has been paused while the world around me continues to move on. The glimmer of hope that he is alive in that rubble is fanned like a flame by this first sunrise. It doesn't seem so scary or so far-fetched in the daylight.

I'm able to stand and pull it together enough to walk back inside, where my three children are sleeping soundly, tucked safely in their beds. Their childhood innocence keeps them unaware of how much the trajectory of their lives is about to change. I didn't know at the time, but I had survived my first of what would be many nights alone, as a thirty-two-year-old widow. In hindsight, this was the first lesson I learned after the attack on the World Trade Center. The sun *always* rises, no matter how dark the night.

I am reminded of that night often because I purposely rise now, almost every day, at that time to greet the sun. It gives me hope, a symbol that life is both tragic and beautiful, and where I put my attention is what I will see. Now, over twenty years after losing my husband, I don't focus on the fear instilled in me after that event. I focus on what his life, my own experiences, and our shared journey have taught me. I focus on gratitude for having rebuilt my life and having successfully raised three healthy children. I focus on what I have learned—my "truth." I contemplate the incredible community forged upon the bedrock of that shared pain. I embrace my story, honoring that rather than being stuck in it, I have allowed its essence to propel me forward—an alchemical transformation born from the crucible of suffering.

My memories of the events surrounding 9/11 are scattered. Trauma is like that. It tucks away the most painful of memories in all the nooks and crannies of our bodies for safekeeping. They aren't gone. Eventually, they find a way to make you look at them—whether in a dream, through a physical illness, or being triggered by something totally unrelated.

If you have ever suffered a traumatic experience, grief, or deep suffering of any kind, which I am pretty sure every human being has, I know you will relate to what I'm saying. Mostly, what I remember comes to me in what I can best describe as snapshots. I get a quick vision of something accompanied by the story, sensations, and emotions I have attached to that moment. The sunrise is one of those snapshots.

This story is not about being broken. It is about being broken open and growing into the best version of yourself. It provides insight into grief's ability to strip away the layers we build up in our everyday lives, exposing our raw and vulnerable emotions. It reveals our deepest selves by bringing our true feelings to the surface, sometimes in ways that surprise us. Sadness, anger, guilt, and even relief can be overwhelming and challenge our sense of identity and understanding of ourselves. Grief also exposes our vulnerabilities and insecurities. It can make us confront our fears, regrets, and unresolved issues. In the face of loss, we may question our beliefs, values, and purpose in life. We reevaluate our relationships and priorities. Grief forces us to confront our own mortality and the impermanence of life, which can be deeply transformative. It is about learning who you are and what you bring to this world and releasing what you want or need to leave behind. It is about soul-deep healing.

A widely held belief says grief is a force that shatters us, commonly linked with feelings of sadness and depression and supported by the statistics that indicate an increased risk of suicide among the bereaved. However, drawing from scientific research, personal experience, intuition, interviews, and anecdotal evidence, I contend that grief can lead us to our best selves. It presents an opportunity to unearth our authentic identity and craft a life that resonates genuinely with who we are.

I confronted the profound truth of transformation when I lost my husband on that fateful day, 9/11. Perhaps you have experienced this yourself or witnessed its echoes in survivors of various mass violence tragedies or the resilience of our service members recovering from the scars of war. When we are diving into topics like grief and trauma, what matters most is how we see the events we are experiencing.

Beauty lies in the diversity of our perceptions, each a unique kaleidoscope of understanding. The part that will remain the same for everyone is the fact that if you want to turn your pain into power, you need to know all it takes is all you've got. Joseph Campbell called it the Hero's Journey for a good reason. We can all be the heroes of our own lives. We simply need to be strong... and soulful.

I want to create a new paradigm around grief and trauma. Why, you ask? The wisdom gained through my own grief and trauma compelled me to a point where I had an undeniable urge to share. This has been a lifetime evolution for me. I was educated in the physiological side of trauma during my nursing career. Nursing gifted me with opportunities to witness death, dying, and grief in all its many forms.

I have held the hand of the dying while comforting those left behind. It gave me the courage to hold space for those in their darkest hours. For years, I've dedicated myself to collaborating with our military and first responder community, providing support to individuals navigating various levels of trauma, grief, and loss. I am currently a keynote speaker and grief mentor, sharing the story and actionable steps toward healing spelled out in this book.

I have to say this has been a divine journey. I intend to offer a different perspective that guides many away from darkness and fear, leading them onto a path of growth. These current times are calling for it. With COVID-19 lockdowns and deaths, multiple mass violence events, unimaginable addiction and suicide rates, and unprecedented worldwide instability, we are *all* collectively experiencing both grief and trauma.

I want to share the story of my life simply because I am not special. My loss is no different from the losses we all inevitably experience. The difference is in my processing, which is a result of all the experiences that led up to that moment on September 11, when the whole world watched as my crucible unfolded. My most devastating loss and greatest lesson played out in real time in homes all over the world. Now, I want to share where it led me and illuminate how each fragment of my life was a stepping stone, furnishing me with the resilience to endure the unimaginable.

I yearn for others to sense it deep within—the profound truth that beyond seemingly insurmountable pain, our best selves emerge. Through my story, I hope to convey that resilience and growth await on the other side of profound adversity.

Grief and trauma are building blocks in the creation of our most beautiful selves. These building blocks are held together and reinforced by the strength and power of hope. Many have said that hope isn't a plan. In the midst of grief and trauma, we aren't looking for a plan. We are looking for a light. Hope is the light that guides us home—back to our soul, the sacredness and the messy human all housed in this one body.

Pain is our compass. It points us to the places we need to go, the places that require our attention. It holds the container for introspection and self-discovery. It is the catalyst for change.

Change is required not only to survive but thrive after loss. Curiosity opens the door to learning and shows us the next path to take. Trust is the ground beneath us. Trust is necessary to step into this space if we are to move anywhere at all.

What is it that we trust? That's for all of us to figure out. It is both the question and the answer. But grace... grace is the recipe, the step-by-step guide to using this grief as a portal. This is the process. It happens one moment at a time. Each moment carries an immeasurable significance that we often only recognize in hindsight.

Everything matters. Every interaction, every thought, every place, person, or thing that we share space with is part of our experience. None of it is coincidental. The divine nature of energy is to be moving, dancing, and interacting in a way that supports all its pieces. Perfection.

We carry with us all we have ever known to be true. Every experience we have had, up until the significant event that has shocked us into a state where we are defenseless, has prepared us to be able to survive. All the walls are down, every emotion raw and amped up like a live wire. We are pure potential wrapped up in the state of feeling like an empty shell of ourselves.

This book was written for *everyone*. I know this is a bold statement, but the truth is we all suffer grief, trauma, and loss. These events fall on a spectrum. You, hopefully, will not experience something as far-reaching as a terrorist attack in one of the largest cities in our nation. This doesn't mean your loss, grief, or trauma is any less significant.

When trauma and grief are involved, there is no comparing. Our culture tends to want to avoid hard conversations around these topics. A labeling happens. That "poor woman," those "poor kids." This labeling and the looks of pity often make us feel as if we have no choice. We are victims. We may have been victimized, but we do not have to carry the title of victim. We can take our power back.

This book is here to remind you that you have *choices*. You may not have had a choice regarding the experience. You may have even felt powerless. But you have a choice in how it will play out in your life. We will hear from people who have suffered the loss of limbs in war, who have suffered sexual abuse, and who have lost a part of themselves that they will grieve for the better part of their lives.

We will hear from experts who can reassure us that we can live a happy and fulfilling life again—with probably even more purpose and intention than we lived before. I will share with you the top five tools that I used to alchemize my pain into a portal that led me to the most authentic and happiest version of myself. These tools are accessible to anyone, anywhere. No equipment is necessary. A simple desire to feel joy again is all it takes. May my journey be a road map for yours.

PART I
GRIEF

CHAPTER 1

The Reckoning

Two months ago, my husband's body was recovered from the rubble that once was the Twin Towers. I'm in the grocery store shopping for my family. It seems like a survivable day so far. I've gotten up, showered, and stepped out of the house. That alone is a win these days. I am going down the aisles the way I normally would, throwing what we regularly use into the cart:

My favorite shampoo.

Snacks for the kids.

Shaving cream for Jeff.

Full stop. As I am about to let it go flying into the cart, I am slapped with reality. *Jeff isn't here. He doesn't need this anymore. I will never buy him another thing again.* As my trembling arm reaches to put it back on the shelf, I feel the now familiar internal collapse. My stomach contorts itself into a tight knot. The feeling that I have a golf ball wedged in my throat returns.

My breathing comes fast, and it's so shallow I fear I'm suffocating. The tears stream down my face and sting my cheeks. I am standing in the middle of the store feeling unrecognizable in my own body. *This cannot be my life. How is this real? Why am I still in this nightmare?* I am shattered. I leave my cart where it is and walk out. No groceries. I sit in the car and cry my eyes out.

This is grief. It barrels over you like a wave knocking you down, leaving you feeling disoriented and exhausted.

My story of traumatic grief begins on September 10, 2001. Anyone who has experienced a pivotal life event can relate to the delineation that occurs. There is the you and your life before the event, and then there is the you and your life after the event. They are not the same. *You* are not the same. Your family unit may not be the same. Nothing in your life will ever be the same again. After Jeff died, my life felt foreign to me.

Before September 11, my life was ordinary. I was a nurse working at St. Vincent's Medical Center, now Richmond University Medical Center, on Staten Island, where Jeff and I had first met prior to him joining the New York City Fire Department (FDNY). He was a firefighter in Engine 10 located in downtown NYC. The firehouse, with its huge steel doors, sat directly across the street from the Twin Towers. Their company patch read "First Due to the Big One" above a stitched outline of the World Trade Center buildings because the two companies had previously responded to the 1993 bombing in the parking garage of the same building. Residing on Staten Island, our commute across the Verrazano Narrows Bridge provided a spectacular view of the towers as they gracefully emerged along the New York skyline. I had seen it so often that I took the view for granted.

We had three children—Vincent, Tori Rose, and Noah. Ours was a very simple life. We were young, in love, both in demanding, service-related careers, and dreaming of our future.

Our first date was memorable. Jeff and I had decided to unwind at a local pub after our 3:00 p.m. to 11:00 p.m. shifts at the hospital. Duffy's was a staple in the neighborhood. We grabbed a high top, and over our perfectly chilled Budweisers, Jeff threw a question at me that was quite unexpected: "What do you want out of life?" It caught me so off guard that I stumbled to find an answer. He'd managed to render me speechless, the most difficult of tasks.

I was astonished this young, long-haired, twenty-seven-year-old guy, who made his living mopping floors, would ask such a profound question on a first date. In true "haven't worked on myself yet" Denise style, I responded sarcastically, "Maybe a shot of Jamo," and I turned the question back on him.

To my complete amazement, he responded, "To make a difference." There was no hesitation. He had obviously contemplated this before. Without another word, he ordered that shot of Jameson's, and we continued to chat. This was Jeff in a nutshell. That rare balance of quick wit and introspection. He could wax philosophical as easily as he could imitate Jim Carrey. He was unique. I left that date with Jeff's question weighing heavily on my heart.

At that time, I was so busy being a single mom to Vincent and trying to make ends meet that I never asked myself what I wanted out of life. I was just accepting what life was handing me. I hadn't yet learned I had the power to be a cocreator in my dreams. Luckily, I had some divine guidance that always seemed to nudge me in the right direction, and eventually I would listen. Such was the case with Jeff.

I had been in a very short-lived marriage to someone I had dated for a long time. When we divorced, I swore off marriage. My devotion and attention were on my son. The feelings of betrayal and pain that I was carrying from my previous relationship made me very wary of considering a relationship with Jeff. This is what happens when we're hurt and don't acknowledge it. That pain bleeds out into other areas of our lives. If I had it my way, as the relationship with Jeff became more serious, I would've probably chosen to walk away out of fear of being hurt.

The universe, in its generosity, had other plans. When we both worked at St. Vincent's, Jeff would often come visit me on my unit. If a code was called, he would run up and watch me work from a distance as we fervently attempted to save someone's life. I would walk out of the patient's room to him leaning against the wall, one leg bent with his foot resting against it, arms folded across his chest with a big, flirty smile on his face.

"I love watching you work," he would tell me. I couldn't resist him. I found myself listening for the sound of his keychain rattling every time I heard the elevator doors open onto my floor. We began seeing each other more. He was easy to love. Vincent loved him as much as I did. The rest is history.

As I sit here reliving those early days, I am taken aback by how much I knew and how much I didn't know about what my future held. I could see us together in a house, laughing, cooking, enjoying cocktails under the moonlight on a porch, or going on adventures with Vincent, even having more children, maybe traveling. Never once did I see myself burying him at thirty-one. We never envision the painful endings.

Fast forward to the afternoon of September 10, 2001. Jeff is now a firefighter and left for work after picking up our oldest son from school. Vincent, eight years old, had stayed after to audition for the school play. Jeff kissed Tori, now three, and Noah, eighteen months old, goodbye and yelled up the stairs to Vincent, "Bye, buddy! I'm proud of you. See ya tomorrow."

Vincent yelled back, "Love you, Dad!"

We walked to the front door together, and I kissed him goodbye. I watched him as he walked to his car. He tossed the green backpack that he never left home without onto the roof of his old beat-up blue work car. His green eyes squinted in the sun as he looked over at me standing in the doorway of our small home.

He smiled and said, "I love you. I'll call you later," like he always did. The ordinary moments. That was the last time I would ever see his face. I just didn't know it.

Jeff did call later. He called to tell me that he would be staying for the day tour in the morning to cover the shift for someone. Selfishly, I was relieved because that meant I didn't have to do a per diem shift at the hospital the next day. I could stay home with my kids. That phone call was the last time I would hear his voice. I didn't know that either.

That part—the "sucker punch" as I call it—shook me the most. The idea that we never know what the next twenty-four hours hold for us, along with the realization of how fragile life really is. How we always take for granted that we have more time. I went to bed that night without a care in the world. The next day, my entire life was ripped out from under me. This is traumatic grief, a complete loss of control, an unexpected violent decimation of all you know to be true. It shakes the very foundation of your soul, and it leaves an indelible mark.

To this day, my children will attest to the irrational fear I have of something happening to them. We live in a small beach town with a volunteer fire department. We rarely hear sirens. This is very different from when we lived in New York. Every time I hear sirens in our area or see an accident on the parkway, I will text them to make sure they're okay, even though they are young adults of twenty-three, twenty-five, and thirty. My mind goes to the worst-case scenario. These are the scars left by traumatic grief.

Very recently I was receiving acupuncture, and my cellphone rang. I was in a dark, meditative room feeling rapturously Zen-like prior to the ringing. To my own surprise, I felt a sudden tightening in my chest, a feeling of impending doom consuming me. I was scared. I could physically feel my nervous system shift into fight, flight, or freeze. I was shocked by my own reaction.

As I lay there, I started becoming curious about this obviously unwarranted response. I was not in any immediate danger. I also recalled this was not the first time I had experienced this response to a phone call.

A vivid memory emerged into my awareness. I had learned about the attack on the World Trade Center when my father had called to ask where Jeff was. My father worked at Jersey City Medical Center at the time, and his office had a full view of the majestic Manhattan skyline. He had seen the first plane crash into the building and witnessed the inferno created by tons of jet fuel. He called concerned, knowing Jeff's firehouse was nearby.

My initial reaction was not one of fear as I told him that Jeff was at work. His firehouse, Engine10/Ladder 10, a.k.a. Tenhouse, stood in the shadows of the World Trade Center.

I knew his company was first due to the towers, but I trusted in his training, and I knew he would be excited for a big job. I obviously prayed for him to be safe because every job a fireman responds to carries risk of injury and death, but my fear did not go beyond that.

As we spoke, my father uttered with shock in his voice, "Another plane is coming!" In that moment, we knew this was not an accident, and that was the moment fear kicked my body into fight or flight. A feeling of powerlessness creates trauma—the inability to protect, to escape, to fix. Until that moment, twenty-plus years later when that phone rang, I wasn't able to articulate that I felt completely powerless when I knew my husband was on his way into a war zone. This is trauma. That phone call shifted me into a trauma response. It was a trigger.

So many years of therapy—yoga, meditation, breathwork, you name it—yet in the midst of an acupuncture treatment I was triggered. I found that interesting. What was different now was that I wasn't afraid to feel it. It sparked my curiosity because I had learned that if I could follow that trigger and allow it to be an indicator, I could heal a bit deeper. I could rewire my neurobiology by breaking the association between the phone ringing and learning about the attack. This would stop my brain from attempting to keep me safe every time the phone rang.

All the work I had done in the past was serving me well. Although traumatic grief may stay with us, it doesn't have to be debilitating. It can be an impetus for deeper self-exploration and growth. All these years of study and working on myself has taught me that the same twenty-four hours that can hold untold pain can also hold infinite possibility.

The towers fell not long after, taking Jeff with them. They also took me. The Denise who existed a few short hours before no longer was. In her place was emptiness, a shell of a woman devoid of identity and direction. It is not coincidental the word "widow," a title I did not want to accept for a very long time, comes from an Indo-European root meaning "be empty." Empty was exactly what I felt. Nothingness.

The beauty in that is that emptiness is the place of unbounded potential. I didn't know it yet. I would never have believed it back then either. I probably would have told you to fuck off if you tried to tell me that I would be who and where I am today. Not only did it feel impossible. It wasn't what I wanted. I wanted what I had. Grief has its way with us, whether we want it or not. We will all fall victim to it at some point. It is a universal experience. I was not special at all. Grief was about to teach me what a formidable force I could be, but first it would render me completely powerless.

CHAPTER 2

Grief Defined

Grief... It seems to have become somewhat of a catch phrase lately. But what is it exactly? Why is everyone talking about it?

The American Psychological Association (APA) states,

> Grief is the anguish experienced after significant loss, usually the death of a beloved person. Grief often includes physiological distress, separation anxiety, confusion, yearning, obsessive dwelling on the past, and apprehension about the future. Intense grief can become life-threatening through disruption of the immune system, self-neglect, and suicidal thoughts. Grief may also take the form of regret for something lost, remorse for something done, or sorrow for a mishap to oneself.[1]

While that definition is certainly true, I prefer the more holistic and hope filled definition written by David Kessler and Elizabeth Kübler-Ross:

> Grief is the intense emotional response to the pain of a loss. It is the reflection of a connection that has been broken. Most important, grief is an emotional, spiritual,

and psychological journey to healing. There is wonder in the power of grief. We don't appreciate its healing powers, yet they are extraordinary and wondrous. It is just as amazing as the physical healing that occurs after a car accident or major surgery. Grief transforms the broken, wounded soul, a soul that no longer wants to get up in the morning, a soul that can find no reason for living, a soul that has suffered an unbelievable loss. Grief alone has the power to heal.[2]

Grief is a *natural* response to loss. Unfortunately, American society is considered a death-denying culture. In general, we do not like to think about, talk about, or acknowledge death as an inevitable reality. While logically we understand that we will all die someday, it is typically a topic that is uncomfortable and swept under the rug.[3] For this reason, the grieving process is often overlooked. Many people are intimidated by the intense emotions, physical sensations, and cognitive changes that yield the power to change a person's way of navigating day-to-day life for some time. Grief is characterized by feelings of sadness, despair, denial, anger, guilt, loneliness, and longing. These emotions are not only normal, but they are a necessary part of the grieving process.

A person in the throes of grief may experience physical sensations such as headaches, muscle tension, fatigue, loss of appetite, digestive issues, and sleep disturbances. The feeling of a "broken heart" is real. I experienced it. During the first few months of my grieving process, I felt a stabbing pain in the area of my heart, and breathing was difficult. Along with the broken heart, brain fog and other cognitive issues—such as the ability to concentrate, make decisions, and remember things—are commonplace. Grief can disrupt our sleep patterns, leading to insomnia, nightmares, or excess sleepiness. Some people may experience loss of appetite and weight loss while others may engage in emotional eating and gain weight. Grief is physically and emotionally draining. It weakens our immune system and makes us more susceptible to illness. Grief is not simply an emotional experience. It reaches into the deepest areas of our mind, body, and soul.

In the chapter that delves more deeply into trauma, you'll notice striking parallels between the responses to grief and trauma. This similarity stems from the fundamental disruption of the nervous system at the heart of grief and trauma. Often, grief can provoke the resurgence of preexisting trauma symptoms or trauma-related disorders, such as PTSD. This resurgence typically happens when the loss evokes memories of past traumatic experiences in an individual.

Traumatic grief, the double whammy, is the tumultuous aftermath triggered by an unforeseen or violent loss. In this complex scenario, not only does the individual grapple with the weight of grief, but they are also thrust into the vortex of trauma. The common phases of shock and denial, typical in any loss, take on an extended duration when the loss is deemed traumatic. Trauma operates as a thief, robbing us of our sense of safety and control and leaving behind a lingering anticipation of impending disaster—that "waiting for the other shoe to drop" feeling, even in the sanctity of our living rooms.

This was the case on September 11. What began as a perfect fall day with an incredibly blue, cloudless sky changed the trajectory of my entire life. It changed the trajectory of our nation. More recent examples of traumatic loss that are wreaking havoc on our communities almost daily are mass violence events, suicides, the drug crisis and accompanying overdoses, loss due to COVID-19, the lingering effects of war, and sex trafficking. The list is endless. These events contribute to the declining mental health in our country and especially in our children.

Traumatic loss can have profound and lasting effects on communities. The immediate impact is, of course, the loss of lives and injuries. These losses reverberate through families and into communities, creating a destabilizing effect. Beyond that, there's often a heightened sense of fear and vulnerability compounded by eroded trust. We, as a nation, are experiencing collective traumatic grief. It is why grief is finally becoming a conversation and why the tools in this book are so valuable.

Beyond traumatic grief, various forms of grief exist, such as normal, anticipatory, complex, cumulative, prolonged, disenfranchised, collective, and more. I've chosen to center this book on traumatic grief due to my personal journey with it. Although we as humans love to create categories and keep things in neat little boxes, nothing in life is black and white. While traumatic grief may be the focus, know that differing types of grief may occur simultaneously. For example, my loss of Jeff was not my first loss or traumatic event. Therefore, I was concurrently experiencing traumatic grief and cumulative, complex, and collective grief.

Over the past two decades, our community, as a collective, has grappled with events that have left a subtle yet pervasive imprint of traumatic grief. Acknowledging and addressing this undercurrent is crucial. By navigating our experiences of traumatic grief in a constructive and healing manner, we can actively contribute to the overall well-being of our community.

Grief, often synonymous with death, extends beyond those somber moments. It accompanies any loss—whether it's a job, a relationship, our health, or even our cherished possessions. The spectrum of grief is vast, ranging from fleeting and subtle to profoundly transformative experiences. Surprisingly, many of us navigate various forms of grief regularly, sometimes without recognizing it. Losing something as seemingly trivial as a favorite necklace elicits grief, though not on the same scale as profound losses like the end of a relationship or the death of a loved one. These diverse experiences coexist on the spectrum of grief.

Grief is not confined to the individual; it extends to the collective and community levels. Events like 9/11 and the ongoing impact of the COVID-19 pandemic exemplify this collective grief. September 11 was not only a personal loss to me. It was also a collective loss to our nation.

The undeniable energy of grief and trauma caused by COVID-19 really lit the fire for me to get this book written and published. While I hadn't personally lost someone to the virus, witnessing the pain of loved ones not being able to be at the bedside of dying family members and the grief in the eyes of masked healthcare workers who felt helpless in the face of a novel virus felt eerily familiar.

People living in fear, the search for answers, and the glorification of normal people doing extraordinary deeds earning the label of hero, even the clapping and cheering for healthcare workers brought me back to the fall of 2001. During the pandemic, we collectively mourned the loss of millions of people as well as ordinary life, grappling with restrictions and facing financial setbacks. We grieved together, but I never heard one person acknowledge that. No one recognized the grieving process that was happening in real time.

Additionally, events like school shootings and mass violence occurring almost daily serve as catalysts, prompting us to confront the communal grief that often goes unacknowledged. While this book focuses on traumatic grief, it also recognizes its pervasiveness and the need for collective acknowledgment and healing.

Irrespective of the form grief takes, the crucial understanding lies in its inherently individual and nonlinear nature. This means we all grieve in our own way and along our own timeline. I can't stress this enough, because often we feel as if we should have "moved on by now." I say absolutely not! As we unravel different parts of ourselves, as we continue on with our lives, we will have moments when grief decides to show up front and center, like an unexpected pedestrian emerging in front of your car prompting an emotional brake slam.

I spent many years pushing that away, praying it wouldn't happen because I was afraid I would become that earlier paralyzed version of myself. Now, when grief rears her head, I welcome her. I invite her in. I let her wash over me, and I feel the sorrow, the emptiness, the melancholic "I wish you could be here" moment. Then, intentionally, I shift my focus to gratitude—gratitude for what was and what presently is. This shift is a conscious choice, a practice that has transformed my relationship with grief. I share my journey with the hope it may resonate with others, offering a different perspective on embracing and navigating the complexities of grief. Discovering what the elixir is for each of us *is* the journey.

Though we will dive deeper into trauma, a brief explanation is necessary here. The hallmark of trauma is the dysregulation of the nervous system. Trauma, similar to grief, comes in many different forms—physical trauma, combat-related trauma, secondary trauma, vicarious trauma. What makes it "traumatic" is the way a person experiences a specific event, *not* the event itself.

What traumatizes me may not traumatize you. Jumping out of a plane would traumatize me. Some people do this for a thrill. It is important to recognize this because it explains the differences in response among individuals during stressful events. It reminds us to have a nonjudgmental attitude toward others and encourages self-reflection around our own reactions in specific situations. Once more, it underscores that the journey of healing and integrating grief is both individual and nonlinear, a crucial understanding we'll continue to explore.

CHAPTER 3

What Is a Memory, What Is a Nightmare?

It has now been over twenty years since my husband was killed in a terrorist attack. I say it that way purposefully. It is a reminder to me that he didn't simply disappear, which is how I feel most of the time. One moment he was here with his wide smile and contagious laughter, and the next he was gone. No warning. No time to say goodbye. No chance to see him one last time. He was torn away from us.

In the days that followed, I experienced an interesting phenomenon. I was awakened to the dissonance between my head and my heart, or the intellectual and the intuitive. My head held on to hope by being in denial. My brain was incapable of accepting what I can best describe as a deep inner knowing. Today, thanks to the teachings of my mentor and friend Lorraine Pickering, I call this deep inner knowing my withinity, or soul wisdom. This part of me recognized my husband was gone.

In these early days, the denial of my inner knowing was necessary because accepting it felt like betrayal and giving up.

Instead, my brain focused on believing in the voids left behind by the pancake effect of the broken buildings. It believed in the survival skills of my husband, who had been trained by one of the best fire departments in the world as well as being an avid outdoorsman. It believed it was impossible for thousands of people to disappear into air thick with concrete, molten steel, and jet fuel—or worse, buried alive.

Hidden beneath the denial and the powerful intellectual argument presented by my brain was the painful truth, the whisper: He was gone. When that thought would find a way to peer out from under all the lies I was telling myself, it paralyzed me. I physically couldn't breathe. The heaviness of it hurt. My chest *hurt*... my heart *hurt*... my head *hurt*... Alluding to that one thought of Jeff being gone created a firestorm of painful energy that was more than emotional.

It was physical. Nothing could relieve it since it was as if someone took a huge oil drill and positioned it directly above my heart space and then turned it on, excavating all I knew to be true and draining me of all the falseness I wanted to cling onto, leaving me crumpled—not dead, but not living.

I had never felt something so agonizing. The days and weeks of waiting, not knowing for certain that he was dead or alive, felt as if I was suspended in some type of purgatory. I would dig through the pockets of Jeff's clothes looking for something I couldn't describe—proof that he had been here. Proof that he had lived and loved and laughed.

Some days I questioned whether it had all been a dream—him, us, our lives... the planes flying into the building... him being buried under 120 stories of rebar and glass, concrete and paper, men and women... love and hate... fear and courage... What was reality? What was fabricated? What was a memory? What was a nightmare? Our brains work in a very disconnected way when we are faced with trauma and overwhelming grief. It goes to great lengths to protect us. Time and reality become distorted. Then I would discover something as simple as a forgotten Home Depot receipt in the pocket of his worn-out jeans. A wave of relief would wash over me. He was here. We were real.

This rush of relief would immediately be followed by the crash of reality that he was gone. I was alone. I felt as if every nerve was exposed and ravaged by a current similar to the third rail. This energy took on a life of its own. This dance that was happening between the knowing and the not knowing went on for almost two months, all encompassing.

My body couldn't handle the enormity of the pain. I didn't have the tools at the time to handle it. Even if I did, I am not sure I would have been able to use them effectively in the immediate aftermath. Tears were not enough. Keeping myself awake for days on end was not enough. My body needed to empty out all that it felt, and the only way it knew how was by physically trying to rid itself. I vomited constantly. When I got updates of any kind from those sifting through the rubble of Ground Zero, also known as "the pile," I would sneak away and throw up. If I looked at my children and felt the fear of not being able to protect them from this pain, I threw up.

Multiple times a day I was on my knees in front of the toilet, some primitive existential prayer, trying to save myself. Energy... unbridled anguish unable to be processed in any logical way. It moved up and out. This violent release created a momentary, deafening silence. The silence was the void. Teetering on the edge of this is where you feel the energy of loss most profoundly. You're afraid to be consumed by it yet afraid to turn away from it lest you forget the person you love. There is nowhere to go. You're trapped.

For the entire first year, I can now say I was dissociated and disconnected from my own body and my feelings. I was a shell of myself. I went through the motions. Holidays, birthdays, ordinary days—I did the best I could to numb and ignore the heavy, paralyzing energy of loss. I honestly didn't think I would survive. It took every ounce of my strength to tend to the basic needs of my children every day. Simple tasks, such as cooking, seemed like a monumental accomplishment. When I was able to do that, you could forget about cleaning the dishes. It wasn't uncommon for them to sit on the table until the next morning unless a friend stopped by and cleaned up for me.

All day long I would feel exhausted. Nighttime would come, and sleep would evade me. It became a cycle of being awake the better part of two to three days and then collapsing out of physical inability to stay awake any longer. I was against any kind of medication. The idea of taking pills frightened me. Alcohol was more familiar, and I tried to drown myself in it occasionally, but a hangover with three kids the next day was harder than the grief I felt being sober. The moments of joy and happiness that would find a way to sneak in were immediately followed by guilt and the fear I was forgetting my husband. Dissociation. Depersonalization. Numbing. Moving out of habit. Doing only what needed to be done. This was how I got through the early days of being a widow. I can barely remember it at all. I was bleeding like a leaky dam, the energy of loss draining my own vitality.

During the initial year following the loss of my husband, I navigated a series of secondary losses, often invisible to those untouched by such deep sorrow. This journey was marked by a seismic shift in my own identity. I mourned the person I was and the shared future I had envisioned with Jeff. The sacrifice of my career, a decision made to nurture my traumatized children, further added to my challenges.

Additionally, I witnessed the unexpected yet not unusual fading of numerous relationships, each loss intensifying my grief. Among these losses, the erosion of my privacy was particularly burdensome. The 9/11 attacks, a national tragedy, inadvertently placed my personal grief on public display.

This relentless scrutiny felt like an intrusion, as if the nation had taken a seat in my living room to observe my family's pain. Grieving publicly brought an added complexity to an already unbearable situation. Simple acts, like picking up my son from school, became ordeals, laden with stares and whispers. Reporters and journalists seemed omnipresent, with newspapers and news channels scrambling for interviews and stories from families of the fallen. Headlines about 9/11 widows started to make front page news. The line between informing the public and exploiting personal tragedy for viewership was blurred.

Jeff was a NYC firefighter. The FDNY had the largest coordinated rescue response and the largest collective loss of all the first responder communities: 343 men. Our home, which should have been a sanctuary of memories and solace, felt besieged by the public's hunger for hero narratives. The label "hero" was branded into my psyche, yet to me he was simply Jeff—my partner, my best friend. To our children he was Dad, irreplaceable and deeply missed.

I fought to keep Jeff's memory close to protect him, our relationship, and our children from what was an overwhelming invasion of our privacy. I wanted our story to be held sacred and intact and truthful. I did not want it to be spun into a fairy tale that made other people feel better. Initially, I resisted allowing Jeff's photograph to appear in newspapers. I am sure you can conjure up the now infamous image of the 343 that was plastered all over the news.[1] This was not Jeff's style. He was humble and would say he was only doing his job. However, persuaded by a childhood friend of Jeff's, I eventually consented, recognizing that Jeff's sacrifice deserved to be remembered and honored.

This intrusion of our privacy, the hallmark of public grief, became painfully evident forty days later when news of the recovery of Jeff's body was recklessly reported by a newspaper before any official confirmation or notification was made. I received a heart-wrenching call from Jeff's best friend, Danny Poggioli, inquiring if I had heard from the fire department. When I responded in the negative, he reluctantly conveyed the news he had read that morning in a popular daily NY paper. Jeff had been found.

This seemed impossible, as protocol dictated no disclosure of names prior to DNA confirmation and family notification. Frantically, I contacted Jeff's captain, Gene Kielty, who was equally upset I had learned of this through the media. He confirmed the discovery but explained that official notification was delayed due to pending DNA results. I endured a harrowing twenty-four-hour wait for the confirmation and formal notification. During this agonizing period, I began to comprehend the repercussions of grieving in the public eye.

Reflecting on my journey, I smile because I'm struck by the total transformation in my attitude toward sharing our story. What I once guarded zealously as a private tribute, I now feel compelled to share openly with the world. Grief has been my teacher, imparting invaluable lessons. One being that by bringing our hidden sorrows into the light, we strip them of their power to intimidate us and eat us alive. Additionally, by sharing our truths, we inspire others to do the same.

I saw firsthand the significant impact that sharing our story had on people who were suffering from trauma and loss, its potential for healing, and the opportunity it presented to honor and preserve Jeff's legacy. My decision to become a storyteller was not about crafting a story for public entertainment but about faithfully representing the reality of our lives. It was a commitment to safeguard our memories in a manner that felt right to me, one that not only served my healing but also offered comfort and encouragement to others. This path has cemented for me the ancient belief around the transformational power of storytelling being both cathartic and a means of preserving history.

■

CHAPTER 4

The Energy of Grief

Grief and trauma has an energy. Every single thing in our lives, right down to the molecules floating in the air around us in this very moment, has an energy.[1] It isn't something tangible, but you can't deny its existence because you feel it. Have you ever been out in public and noticed someone who made you want to move away from them? They don't even have to be doing anything particularly nefarious. You just have a feeling. Or maybe you have encountered a complete stranger who you were instantly drawn to. What you are feeling is energy... and it is all around us. Every second of every day, it influences how we take in information and process what is happening in our lives. We absorb and contribute to collective energy with every thought, emotion, and action.

Numerous forms of energy exist, some of which you might recall from science lessons, including kinetic, potential, nuclear, and gravitational, among others. Interestingly, vibrational energy has been utilized to gauge our emotional states. Vibration, in the context of energy, refers to the movement of particles in a substance or system.[2] Emotions, often considered abstract and intangible, can be viewed through the measurable lens of energy and vibration.

"A groundbreaking study by Dr. David R. Hawkins and the Institute of Noetic Sciences demonstrated the existence of an energy field generated by various emotions, sometimes described as a 'consciousness field.' Using a technique called applied kinesiology, Dr. Hawkins developed a scale that assigned distinct frequency values to different emotions, ranging from shame (20) to enlightenment (700+). Emotions such as fear and anger had lower frequencies, while emotions like love and joy were found to have higher frequencies."[3]

"When we emit emotional energy through our thoughts, feelings, and actions, it has the potential to affect not only us but also those around us. Researchers at the HeartMath Institute have found that the heart generates the most strong electromagnetic field in the human body, which our emotions can influence. Research at the institute shows that feelings of love and compassion can create a synchronized harmony between our heart and brain frequencies, positively influencing those around us. Contrastingly, emotions like anger and frustration can cause an erratic and unsynchronized heart and brain frequency pattern, negatively impacting our environment. Our emotional energy can not only create a ripple effect in our immediate surroundings but may also extend outward, ultimately influencing collective human consciousness. Understanding the power of our emotional energy helps us lead a more authentic and self-aware existence and emphasizes our interconnectedness with the world that surrounds us."[4]

This helps to explain why we are drawn to or repelled by certain people, places, or situations. It also helps explain how grief and trauma have such a marked influence on our physical bodies.

The energy of loss is profoundly deep. On the Hawkins scale of consciousness, grief registers at a mere 75Hz. This is in stark contrast to the vibrational energy of love, which resonates at approximately 500Hz. As the vibration diminishes, a sense of heaviness and stagnation begins to permeate the mind and body, whereas higher vibrations are associated with a feeling of lightness and liberation. Grief is an intricate emotion; it is dark, cavernous, and confusing. Its presence is constant and silent, looming over every part of your life. Yet it feels explosively shattering, like the scream in your dream that won't come out. This emotion brings with it a sense of hopelessness, a pervasive fear, and an overwhelming heaviness as it methodically deconstructs our sense of self.

I have interviewed people in the course of writing this book, and I always ask them to describe grief or trauma in three words. The answers are eerily similar, regardless of the cause of the trauma or grief. Pam, a victim of military sexual trauma, described it as "shattering, collapsing... it steals everything." Another FDNY widow, Kathleen Ryan, who lost her husband Bobby in a fire, described it as "dismantling." Earl Granville, US Army veteran and amputee, used the word "obstacle." In all cases, the difficulty of surviving the void created by traumatic loss is felt.

When considering trauma and grief, sadness is often perceived as the predominant emotion. While this may be true, sadness is often preceded by denial. Denial always gets a bad rap as being an unhealthy coping mechanism. According to an article written by Elizabeth Kübler-Ross and David Kessler, two well respected grief researchers, "Denial and shock help us to cope and make survival possible. Denial helps us to pace our feelings of grief. There is a grace in denial. It is nature's way of letting in only as much as we can handle."[5]

My brain automatically went into a protective mode that only allowed me to process certain details about my experience. This denial was freaking necessary. It would determine my emotional response. Denial was the key to the slow and more digestible disintegration of my internal structure. If the process went any quicker, it would have meant a complete collapse of my being. By slowly moving toward acceptance, I was able to heal layer by layer. Space was created for all the emotions that accompany loss to move through me.

While it is commonly understood that grief manifests as emotional distress, its impact is not solely psychological. It also exerts a considerable physical strain. This is evidenced in the studies conducted supporting the measurable physical vibrations of our emotions. Through my years of observation and experience, I have grown to understand that both loss and grief deeply and persistently influence our nervous system, especially in cases of traumatic grief. Our stress response is triggered at the time of the initial event. This may result in extreme fatigue, chest pain and shortness of breath, lowered immunity leading to susceptibility to illness, body aches and pains, digestive issues, and brain fog, to name a few.[6] My dear friend Pam, an Army veteran, described her traumatic grief as "a roller-coaster. You don't know what any day is going to bring. If you're not fully present, you're numb. No in between." In my opinion, the only way we can heal from any trauma or loss is by becoming intimately acquainted with our own nervous system responses and learning how to regulate those responses.

How does one endure and overcome the emotional and physical repercussions of grief? We each adopt unique approaches to navigating our loss. The aim for all of us as humans is to protect ourselves, and this is done through our nervous system response. Typically, we begin by relying on the strategies we've used throughout our lives—our instinctive, default mechanisms. These habits, often developed in early childhood, are not generally the healthiest methods for managing loss or other challenges. They are quite reflexive and often informed by the survival reactions of those around us, such as our parents. These responses tend to be effective only for a short period of time, after which they then begin to do more harm than good. The early period of unintentional reaction is what I refer to as our survival mode. My survival tool was dissociation.

In his book, *The Body Keeps the Score: Brain, Mind, and Body in the Healing of Trauma*, Bessel van der Kolk explains that dissociation serves as a survival strategy when individuals are unable to escape or fight back during traumatic events. He states, "Dissociation is a reversible reaction to feeling trapped, overwhelmed, and helpless. It can occur in response to physical or emotional pain or in situations of extreme stress."[7]

Van der Kolk further elucidates that dissociation can manifest in various forms, such as dissociative amnesia, where individuals have gaps in their memory surrounding the traumatic event, or depersonalization, where individuals feel detached from their own bodies and emotions.[8]

While dissociation can be protective at times, in the long run it disrupts daily activities, making it difficult to focus, remember tasks, or engage in social interactions. This can affect performance at work, school, and in personal relationships. It can lead to a sense of detachment from one's feelings, making it difficult to experience joy, sadness, or other emotions fully. This hinders your overall quality of life. When you numb the pain, you numb the joy. Dissociation can serve as a barrier to processing and healing from traumatic events, as it prevents individuals from fully confronting and working through their experiences. This is not a tool that we would utilize if we were looking to fully recover from trauma and loss.

Both Pam and Earl, Army veterans who have battled different forms of traumatic loss, describe the negative healing modalities they used prior to finding the tools that truly helped them find themselves. Drugs, drinking, sex, excessive working out—anything that would help them *numb* the pain and forget the reality. Though not healthy nor sustainable, these temporary escapes helped them to stay alive. These survival tools kept them here long enough to find healthier coping skills. Their stories are not uncommon.

Active healing cannot happen when we are in a state of denial or using tools of avoidance. These simply allow us to survive, and survival is the name of the game in the beginning. Judgment (of ourselves, of others, or by others) should have no place in the healing journey. We do what we need to do to get by until we can do better. Some days I didn't want to get better. The future was bleak at best and nonexistent at worst. I ached to be wherever Jeff was.

"Just get through today," I would say over and over... "Smile so the kids don't know you're sad. Don't cry because you will frighten them. Save the tears for when you are alone in the shower. Remember how he would poke his head in every single time you were showering, and you would complain that you didn't get a minute alone, or you would laugh because he could never seem to get enough of you? Is he looking at me now in the shower, snotty crying, and being a shitty mom?" So many irrational thoughts, so many memories that feel like glass shards to my brain, so many words trapped in the constriction of my throat. This is what loss feels like.

The energy of loss is not comprised solely of your own pain and suffering. It includes the actions and emotions of everyone around you. Even those with the best intentions can contribute to a feeling of overwhelm. In an effort to console, people often say the most hurtful, ignorant things such as, "Time heals all things," or, "He is in a better place." For me, it was the way I would see people looking at me. It reminded me of the way I would strain my neck to look at a car crash on the highway. You feel people's fears of ever having to walk in your shoes. You sense the pity.

I, somehow, took on the responsibility of trying to manage other people's grief. I didn't do this intentionally. I am a protector by nature. I didn't want them to become sadder by looking at me. I tried my best to be the *strong* widow. This was a fruitless endeavor. I had no control over anyone else's feelings at the time. I barely had control over my own. All it did was leave me exhausted and filled with resentment and repressed emotions.

I learned early on that grief is a magnifier. Anything you are becomes greater in the energy of loss. Any strengths you have are fortified. Any weaknesses you have are exploited. This didn't just happen on an individual level. It happened on the family level and the greater community level. We witnessed the best and the worst in everyone. This added another level of complexity and debilitation to my experience. Pam echoed my experience of multi layered grief after trauma. She described it as "a loss of myself. My career. Losing a whole community that was supposed to be more like family than a job. Betrayal..."

While I was bombarded by people wanting to hear my story, Pam had a completely opposite experience. She couldn't get anyone to acknowledge what had happened to her. She was shrouded in shame and isolation. The Department of Veterans Affairs (VA) estimates that one in three women and one in fifty men who've served in the military have experienced MST (defined as sexual assault or sexual harassment during military service).[9] The military's culture of secrecy can lead to survivors enduring the aftermath of sexual assault on their own, without the support and therapy that could otherwise help them cope with the resulting distress.[10] Whereas Jeff's fire department family soon became my family, Pam was ostracized. Pam lost her career, friends, and her sense of safety.

When we experience any kind of trauma, we expect that certain people, usually those closest to us, will be at our doorstep to support us. The reality is that during these times we learn who we can depend on. Often those we believed would be our pillars of strength are nowhere to be found. It is confusing and disheartening when this happens. The feeling of loss is compounded by betrayal and other extraneous losses. Yet this is a gift. You learn to surround yourself with people who lift you up. You tighten your circle. You find your tribe.

Pam found her tribe after hearing another survivor of MST on a podcast sharing her story. This brave woman spoke openly about her experience and about the healing benefits of service dogs. Pam knew immediately they needed to meet. Eventually, Pam was approved for a service dog and was able to meet the woman who had spoken to her pain on the podcast in person. Pam was welcomed into the flock and immediately felt as if she had found her tribe. Pam credits both Nimitz, her service dog, and her newfound community with restoring her ability to live in the moment.

Trust me when I say, for every person who lets you down and falls away, the universe provides an unexpected angel just when you need it. At speaking engagements, people always laugh when I say that sometimes the trash takes itself out. It may sound crude, but believe me. It's true. Trust the falling away of certain people. The good ones always stay.

Earl became one of the change-makers. He hit rock bottom after not only losing his leg in combat but also losing his twin brother to suicide. He chose to isolate himself and do anything to numb the pain. He found healing in the phrase he coined "The Three Ps": purpose, passion, part of something. He plays an influential role in many nonprofits that serve the veteran community as well as being a national keynote speaker.

The energy of loss brings you to your knees. I felt as broken as I could ever be, buried alive by pain. But, as the old saying goes, when life knocks you down to your knees, you're in the perfect position to pray. For me, this is where the healing began. To be honest, after two years of being in this position, I decided I didn't want to live this way. I didn't want the rest of my life to feel as if I was carrying around a ball and chain. I began to intentionally focus on rebuilding and creating a new normal.

Although this book outlines the tools I used to navigate and heal my traumatic grief, it is important you remember grieving is never one size fits all. Take what serves you here and leave the rest.

CHAPTER 5

The Clash of the Past and Present

Every time I hear a story of devastating, traumatic loss, my heart feels heavy for those left behind to walk this path of grieving. I find myself wondering how they will endure. I wonder, *How could they possibly sleep? Are they able to eat? Does their house offer comfort or feel like a prison?* I forget, momentarily, that I have walked that path and come out the other side. I find myself in awe of the amount of pain a human can endure. I am reminded of all that goes into this journey that takes you down into the depths of your own soul on the path from hopeless to hopeful.

Prior to losing Jeff and the life we had planned together, I had not connected the dots in my life. I had no appreciation for my struggles and past losses. They seemed random and unrelated. They served no purpose that I could discern, other than leaving me feeling resentful, angry, victimized, and sorry for myself. The idea that everything in my life is here to serve me would have sounded like a bunch of horse crap to me, a lame excuse, and most likely pissed me off. Even more interesting, although I was a nurse and knew how stress played a role in our health, I was not aware of the depth of the mind, body, and soul connection. Gratefully, over the course of the previous thirty-one years, I had been evolving without even knowing it. Throughout my entire life, the scene was being set. I was gaining the tools I would need to survive the darkest times of my life thus far.

I was born to a brave eighteen-year-old woman who had survived unspeakable childhood trauma. She married my father, and they continued the cycle of abuse that had plagued both their families for generations. Their relationship was immature, toxic, and violent. They divorced when I was two, not long after my sister was born. This same year, I developed asthma. The trauma, in my two years on this earth, had already settled in my body.

In traditional Chinese medicine (TCM), emotions are deeply interconnected with the body's organs and their corresponding energy pathways. Each emotion is linked to specific organs, and grief finds its association with the lungs. According to TCM principles, when grief remains unexpressed or unresolved, it can disrupt the flow of qi (life force) within the lungs, leading to an imbalance. This imbalance might manifest as symptoms such as respiratory problems like asthma or recurring coughs.[1]

I mention this because TCM will play a tremendous part in my healing as my story progresses. I was a two-year-old who didn't have the capacity to express and resolve the complex grief she was experiencing on multiple levels—fear, trauma, abandonment, loss. Western medicine wrote my asthma off to genetics. Although a person is more likely to develop asthma if they have a family history, no gene has been found to lead to it. What is fascinating is the established connection between asthma and post-traumatic stress disorder (PTSD). Research in the *European Respiratory Journal* revealed that individuals with PTSD are three times more likely to develop asthma compared to those without it.[2] Similarly, the Asthma and Allergy Foundation of America conducted a study indicating a heightened risk of asthma in PTSD patients, especially those under the age of twenty.[3]

When I was eleven, I experienced the gaping loss of my grandmother, a cornerstone of my existence. She was the stability in my life. For years, when I was spending sporadic weekends with my father, I slept at her house. She was not just a guardian; she was my example of conviction and compassion.

My grandmother had unwavering faith. Her nightly ritual of blessing us with holy water after prayers for our family was a testament to this faith. Accompanying her to church, I was allowed the simple joy of playing at her feet while she devoutly recited the rosary. Her generosity knew no bounds, always ready to offer whatever little she had to those in need. She was an avid reader and lover of mysteries, with Agatha Christie being one of her favorites. She took me to the library, taught me to write my name well enough to get a library card, and we would take out stacks of books.

Back then, I couldn't fully grasp the values she was instilling in me through her modest, faithful living. Yet the sense of security and belonging I felt in her presence was undeniable. I can still recall the way she would gently tuck my messy hair behind my ear when she would speak to me and the way she poured her tea from the cup into the saucer to drink.

Her passing marked a turning point in my life. When she died, I had my first lasting experience of intuition. It was a school day, and I had an unsettled feeling. The intensity was strong enough that when my sister and I got off the school bus, I told her we should run home. I was greeted by my mother crying in the kitchen. What I remember most about that time was my inability to cry. I was so sad. I was worried about what my life would look like without her. But I couldn't cry. Strangely, in the face of such sorrow, I found myself unable to shed a single tear, as if I had already mastered the art of emotional detachment. In lieu of crying, I turned to physical exertion, seeking solace in the rhythm of sit-ups, as if to physically push away the grief that threatened to overwhelm me. This coping mechanism revealed an early lesson in resilience.

My teenage years, like most, were a mix of turmoil and the type of fun you only experience when you're young, adventurous, and naive. As a diligent student, I often wrestled with feelings of inadequacy despite my accomplishments. My education took place in a prestigious all-girls Catholic high school, known for its stringent entry criteria. Yet being placed in the second academic track left me feeling decidedly ordinary amid a sea of exceptional peers. I was athletic but never felt confident enough to continue playing sports.

I started pushing boundaries and becoming rebellious in my search of myself. This phase of testing limits inevitably led to a strained relationship with my parents. In retrospect, I recognize that my actions may have inadvertently stirred unresolved issues within my mother, whose protective responses, though rooted in concern, often felt to me like contempt and mistrust. This fueled my fire for independence.

Amid these trials, like many teens, I harbored a deep-seated desire for popularity—a goal I achieved but not without cost. In the pursuit of social standing, I regrettably embodied the stereotype of the "mean girl," often at the expense of kindness toward those outside my immediate circle. This reflection on my adolescent behavior serves as a reminder of the complexities of growing up, where the pursuit of acceptance can sometimes lead us astray from our truest selves.

This is where I believe the intentional separation begins. In our quest to fit in, we ignore our personal gifts and our truest desires, and we attempt to become like everyone else. This inevitably leads to unhappiness and lack of satisfaction in our lives.

The truth is that I don't remember much about my childhood. I don't remember many birthdays or holidays. I look at pictures of my younger self, and she feels like someone else. Trauma does this to us. It acts as a veil, obscuring memories and altering perceptions. Trauma embeds within us a unique survival mechanism, a sort of internal operating system designed to navigate through the vulnerabilities of childhood, especially when we find ourselves ensnared in situations beyond our control or understanding.

When I was twenty-three, I married someone who was also marred by unprocessed grief and trauma. His mother died when he was sixteen, and we met a few short years after. Our relationship felt familiar to me. It was filled with the chaos, the fighting, and the lack of communication I grew up with. Rather than be disconcerted by this, I was drawn in by the comfort created by familiarity. I thought this dysfunctional behavior was normal.

I discovered his drug use before we were married. I had no knowledge of addiction, even though I was surrounded with it in various forms throughout my life. I thought if I tried harder, if I loved him enough, he would change. He tried. Then I got pregnant, and we got married. I naively believed that being a father and husband would make him happy, and he would no longer need to get high. Of course, I was wrong.

The stress of marriage and a child only exacerbated his addictive behaviors. He became abusive—financially, physically, and emotionally. I spent countless hours trying to stay one step ahead of him, playing detective, hiding money, and protecting my son. Finally, after one particularly frightening event, I decided I needed to leave. Nothing I could do would change him. While he was out of the house, I packed up a few things for myself and my son and left. I spent a year living with my parents. I saved up enough money to get an apartment and begin a new life. As I said earlier, I did not acknowledge my grief. I was caught up in the anger and the day-to-day tasks of being a single mother. I lived by the motto "do what you have to do," and in the process, I compartmentalized that pain too.

At this point, I had sworn off men and marriage like many a scorned woman. Fortunately, the universe likes to throw us curveballs to make sure we're still in the game. I met Jeff about two years later. Much like our first date, our relationship continued in a similar fashion of learning and laughter. He taught me how to communicate openly in one single sentence.

Following my divorce, which intensified my feelings of abandonment, I took great pride in my transformation into a fiercely independent woman, no longer reliant on a man for support or happiness. I could handle life on my own. I proved that to myself by providing a life for me and my son that was happier than any other time I could remember. While we were dating, Jeff and I had a difference of opinion on a topic I can't even recall (that's how unimportant it was). After some back and forth in the conversation, I basically told him if he didn't like the way I was doing something, he was welcome to leave. By that time, I had grown so accustomed to being left behind, both physically and emotionally, by men that I thought suggesting he leave first would be my safeguard against any hurt. His response was so simple.

"Dee, just because we disagree on something doesn't mean I'm leaving you."

It hit a nerve. Even writing this brings up a visceral reaction. It seems so straightforward, but it never occurred to me that we could openly express our differences and love each other in spite of them. I had never loved or been loved that way before. I was never permitted to simply state a difference of opinion without creating an emotional firestorm or being completely dismissed. This changed me fundamentally. It felt safe, it felt honest, and it was liberating!

Why the trip down memory lane? All of these seemingly unrelated experiences created perceptions, behaviors, and responses that determined my thoughts and reactions in the midst of the crisis following September 11.

Let's return to the physical manifestations. Initially, I was unaware of the connection between my body, mind, and soul. However, the pieces of the puzzle began to fit together when I reflected on my past. My parents' divorce occurred around the same time as my asthma onset. I also suffered from eczema, which in traditional Chinese medicine is related to an imbalance in the lungs. Further introspection led me to notice a pattern: Intense emotional episodes, such as the events surrounding 9/11, often resulted in a tightness in my chest, necessitating reliance on an inhaler or a flare-up of my eczema. For over twenty years, I had been unknowingly harboring trauma and grief in my body, which, coupled with the stresses of losing Jeff, raising children, and managing a household solo, had a significant impact on my endocrine and immune systems.

Grief and trauma are stored in our bodies, most problematically our nervous system, which governs the reactions of all our bodily systems.

A notable observation is that conventional medicine never took into account my traumatic life experiences in its treatment approach, which proved ineffective for me. Eventually, my eczema was out of control and severely impacted my quality of life. According to my Western practitioners, there is no cure, and the only treatment was high doses of steroids that further depleted my body, and when the course of treatment was completed, the eczema would come back worse than ever. Only upon consulting alternative and complementary health practitioners was the link between my physical ailments and my past traumas recognized and appropriately addressed, leading to effective treatment.

Similarly, my youngest son, Noah, experienced this distinct expression of grief. He developed severe eczema and struggled with food allergies, which I initially thought were isolated health issues. However, with a deeper insight into his situation, I've come to understand these conditions as integral to his process of grieving. Noah was less than two years old during a period of significant loss in our family. At such a tender age, he was incapable of fully understanding or expressing the profound feelings associated with this loss. Consequently, his body seemed to internalize and manifest this unprocessed grief and trauma through physical symptoms.

This realization highlights the often overlooked but powerful impact of emotional experiences on physical health, particularly in children who may not have the capacity to verbally express their emotions. My daughter suffered from insomnia at three years old. She also developed anxiety that took me a little bit of time to realize because it presented through incessant yawning. I hadn't known that incessant yawning was a common symptom of anxiety and a trauma response. I thought it was because she was tired or bored. It persisted for many years until we learned the correlation. Vincent was older and more understanding of his loss. He briefly went to therapy and was diagnosed with PTSD and generalized anxiety disorder at the age of eight.

The emotional impacts of my prior life experiences did not show up as memories. They showed up as behaviors. As an adult, I had learned I was an introverted extrovert. I like being around people, but I keep my deepest emotions to myself. After being around a crowd of people, I require down time to reset. While I appreciated the support, I would long for time away from the crowds of people who were at my house in the early weeks of waiting.

Not surprisingly, I refused to cry in front of people. The level of pain I was experiencing after the collapse of the buildings was hard to hide, but tears and breaking down were not my default. The shower and my bed were my safe places for tears. In front of people, crying created a feeling of shame and weakness.

I recall about five years into my grieving process regretting not falling to the ground or allowing myself to release that guttural scream that had built up in my belly in those first few weeks, because at five years, I wanted to do it. At that point, most people expect you to have moved past the acuteness of your grief, and I figured someone would want to commit me if I decided to scream and cry. This compartmentalization of feelings remains a vulnerable aspect for me, a work in progress. I am better at crying. I intentionally worked on it. We are all works in progress. That makes us human. Some lessons are harder to learn.

My perspective on relationships has also been significantly shaped by my experiences. I always find it interesting that one of the first questions I am inevitably asked at speaking engagements is if I am dating or remarried. For the record, I have never remarried. I have dated in the past, but I find myself most comfortable being single. After years of therapy, I can say I still have some unresolved abandonment issues, and my fierce independence is indicative of an attachment style that is more prone to being alone. Both have been sculpted by the events I shared previously.

While this may be true, I prefer to believe that, over the course of twenty years of self-awareness, reflection, and choosing to honor the desires of my soul, I have curated a life that truly nourishes me. My dear friend, Lieutenant Dan Murphy, who retired out of Rescue 2 in Brooklyn after thirty-six years of dedicated service to the city of New York, once said to me that it seems as if I've compensated for Jeff's absence by surrounding myself with remarkable individuals who collectively embody what he represented in my life. It struck a deep chord. I am still very independent, but if 9/11 taught me anything, it was the power of community and asking for help when I need it.

One of the immediate responses one has to a traumatic loss is a questioning of faith. Raised in the Catholic tradition, I initially turned to my religious roots for comfort after Jeff's passing, only to find it lacking. The gap between my grief and the church's doctrines was disheartening, leaving me with more questions than answers. Yet my faith in God and the Blessed Mother never wavered. For my entire life, no matter what was happening, I prayed. I trusted that I was held and protected. Prayer was my constant refuge, a practice ingrained in me since childhood, inspired by my grandmother's unwavering devotion. In fact, my aunt gave me my grandmother's rosary to comfort me in the weeks following my loss. Although I strayed from traditional practices like attending Mass, my prayers were fervent, born from a place of necessity. I prayed as if my life depended on it because at times it did.

This journey forced me to scrutinize my spiritual and religious beliefs, seeking what resonated with my soul—a path familiar to many who endure profound loss. The inevitable question arises: "Where was God in my suffering?" We all need to find the answer to this question ourselves. For me, such introspection solidified my faith, leading me to trust that everything in life, even the most painful experiences, were divinely orchestrated and serve a purpose. I've come to view these hardships as gifts in shitty wrapping paper.

Culturally, many customs and traditions surround grief and loss. Mourning is the outward expression of our grief. As I stated earlier, mourning rituals help us accept and acknowledge our loss, and they provide a platform for our community to support us. But that isn't the only way our culture plays into grief. I was raised in an Italian household.

Meals are sacrosanct to us. The whole family gathered at the dinner table. It was important to me that we all ate together. It was the time when we could check in with each other, discuss our days, laugh together, bitch, and problem solve.

Despite Jeff and me working opposite shifts as a firefighter and nurse, we managed to prepare dinner, sit with the kids, and then spend time together upon returning home from work. After 9/11, I was thrown into chaos, and dinner time was no longer a sit-down type of meal. I did whatever I needed to do to get through the day. I knew if I wanted to create a feeling of "normalcy," I needed to bring back sit-down family dinners. To this day, I clearly remember the first meal I cooked. It was a family favorite—roast beef, mashed potatoes, and corn. Cultural traditions can create a feeling of stability and security, something necessary if we are to feel safe after traumatic loss.

The relationship with a person who passes away stands as one of the most influential factors in shaping our experience of grief. Losing Jeff meant not only losing my husband but also my confidant, my intimate partner, the father of my children, the primary breadwinner, and the embodiment of all my aspirations and dreams.

His unexpected, violent death at the age of thirty-one, despite being perfectly healthy, added a layer of shock to the profound sorrow. The loss of a loved one is always devastating, but when it is not the natural order of things, such as in the loss of a child, an added layer is filled with unrealized dreams and milestones such as first days of school, proms, graduations, and wedding dances.

It's essential to clarify that I'm not comparing traumas or grief. Each experience is uniquely painful and overwhelming. However, what remains universally true is that the nature of our relationship with the deceased profoundly influences the contours of our grieving process and the extent of what we've lost. My children lost their protector. My sons lost the man who would advise them, drive them to practice, cheer at their games, and also keep them in line. My daughter lost the man who would set the bar for all the other men in her life. Not a milestone in our lives happens without the thought of what is missing. Someone recently mentioned to me that when you lose a sibling, you lose a part of your parents also because they lose a part of themselves. That really struck me. The ripple effect of one person's presence is way more far-reaching than we imagine.

The conscious and unconscious factors that affect grief are actually the micro portals to ourselves. I described my emotions immediately after 9/11 as being magnified. If I was feeling grateful for a kind gesture, it was a level of gratitude that could make my heart explode. It helped me understand how kindness can literally save someone's life. The sadness was crippling. Feeling this in the depth of my being created a level of empathy I had never been able to access before. My resilience was at a magnitude that is best described as animalistic, feral… the will to survive and the desire to protect my babies. Everything was *big*. Grief magnifies everything. Traumatic grief will not be overlooked or ignored. It roars in your face. It devours the masks, the imprinting, and the ego and allows who you truly are to finally be seen.

Loss in any capacity requires us to examine all that we have known. In the end, we sift through the rubble and rebuild, using what now aligns with our heart and soul rather than what we accepted in the past, which was most likely what our families, communities, and society deemed as important and necessary. The dismantling quality of grief and the questioning it creates in our lives allows us to discern and connect to our own truth.

CHAPTER 6

Shadows and Light: Factors Influencing Grief

Elisabeth Kübler-Ross, a Swiss-American psychiatrist, introduced a groundbreaking theory on the stages of grief in her 1969 book *On Death and Dying*. The theory, often known as the Kübler-Ross model, outlines five key stages people go through when dealing with grief and loss. This work is historically significant, as it marked a cultural shift in the approach to conversations regarding death and dying.[1] Modern theories on grief, however, have moved away from a "one size fits all" solution to navigating loss. Grief is not linear or uniform, as formerly believed, with "normal" grief and "pathological" grief. Rather, grief falls on a spectrum that defies the notion of standardized stages.[2] The experience of grief is highly individualized, influenced by factors such as personality, attachment style, life experiences, and even genetic makeup.[3] it's important to recognize how certain factors can influence the process.

Having read the short synopsis of my life, you may already be identifying how these prior experiences determined the path I found myself stumbling upon after the death of my husband. By exploring these factors, we can gain a deeper understanding of our own personal reactions and behaviors. This understanding fosters acknowledgment and acceptance, paving the way to connect with the deepest aspects of our authentic selves. Embracing this authenticity can be a transformative experience, allowing us to tap into the well of our true potential. It makes this work so powerful.

When we consider grief, our thoughts often default to the loss of a loved one. However, grief encompasses a broader spectrum of experiences, including the end of a cherished relationship, job loss, infertility, declining health, the aftermath of rape and abuse, or even the loss of a sentimental item. Because the majority of research and information available on grieving centers around bereavement, some people do not even *realize* what they are experiencing after a loss or traumatic experience is grief! They don't understand the intense emotions and often try to ignore them or explain them away instead of acknowledging and honoring them properly. For people to mislabel their grief as depression, anxiety, anger, or even laziness is not uncommon.

In my case, the end of my first marriage, initiated by me, did not bring the anticipated relief but a profound sadness. This sadness, misattributed to personal failure and an inability to "fix" my partner, was, in truth, unacknowledged grief— mourning the loss of a dream, the deterioration of a loved one, and the realization of my own limitations. Only later did I recognize this as a natural response to a significant emotional loss. Transmutation of grief only happens through acknowledgment.

Grief is complex, allowing for the simultaneous experience of countless emotions and reactions. One can feel relief and sorrow concurrently, mourn the past while anticipating the future, and even choose to let go of something while grappling with a profound sense of loss—all within the same emotional space. The crucial initial step toward healing is to recognize and name what you are experiencing as grief.

The depth of our grief correlates with the value we placed on what was lost. While the death of a loved one represents a profound and enduring loss, other losses may evoke transient sadness or frustration that eventually fades. However, losses tied to personal autonomy or choice, such as those stemming from violence or abuse, may require extensive treatment for healing. The greater the influence of the loss on your life, the longer the grief process.

Personality plays a significant role in the grieving process. My journey through grief, marked by a history of trauma, was a testament to this. The pain of losing Jeff was compounded by my innate need to "fix" things, a trait forged from childhood challenges. Give me any problem, and I can find you a solution. When Jeff died, I could do nothing to bring him back or to fix the pain my children were experiencing. This feeling made my grief almost unmanageable. It contributed to the lack of control I was already feeling. If you were prone to depression prior to your loss, you may experience a more difficult grief process. Conversely, it would seem that if you tend to be upbeat, grieving would be less complicated. That may be true; however, we must be careful of the unconscious refusal to acknowledge the loss. Always looking at the bright side can be an avoidance technique where we stay far away from the pain.

Prior to Jeff's dying, I was certainly not someone who always looked at the bright side. In fact, because of traumatic childhood events, I was the type of person who always considered the worst-case scenario and had to have an exit strategy. In the beginning, this part of my personality contributed to the depth of my grief, the feeling of fear that I may unexpectedly lose another person I loved or that something would happen to me, leaving my children without a living parent to care for them. However, in the long run, my "fixer" personality trait motivated me to keep searching for the deepest healing I could find.

Recognizing my insecure attachment style was crucial in understanding my intense response to his loss. Attachment styles, as defined by the *APA Dictionary of Psychology*, are the characteristic ways people relate to others in the context of intimate relationships, which is heavily influenced by self-worth and interpersonal trust. Theoretically, the degree of attachment security in adults is related directly to how well they bonded to others as children.[4] Without getting very complicated, secure attachers tend to display more resilience during heartbreak and take less time to bounce back than insecurely attached individuals. Individuals with unhealthy attachment styles are particularly prone to complicated and prolonged grief, possibly stemming from the PTSD acquired through earlier experiences shaping their attachment style. Complicated grief, also known as prolonged grief, now recognized in the Diagnostic and Statistical Manual of Mental Disorders (DSM) by the American Psychiatric Association (APA), is characterized by intense longings for the deceased or preoccupation with thoughts surrounding the death.[5]

"You seem so strong." I lost count of the number of times I have been told those exact words since Jeff died. I learned through my healing process that, in actuality, I was afraid of being hurt or disappointed, so I wouldn't ask for or accept help. I pushed through by dissociating. Rather than being strong, I was fearful—abandonment issues at their best. You can imagine how losing the person I loved and trusted to never leave me became an emotional tornado very quickly. Even though this was not an intentional abandonment, it cemented a deeply held, unhealthy belief that I would be left without my needs met.

A study by Kristin Glad, a clinical psychologist for the Norwegian Centre for Violence and Traumatic Studies, found that those who experienced traumatic events leading to PTSD were more likely to suffer from complicated grief. The conclusion emphasized that addressing persistent PTSD symptoms could potentially mitigate the development of disabling complicated grief.[6] Given my experience of losing Jeff in a traumatic event and my history of multiple traumas, it's unsurprising I spent eight years in therapy post-9/11.

Grief also intersects with our physical well-being, where our genetic predispositions can either compound or alleviate our suffering. Moreover, age and life stage significantly influence how we process grief. The resilience of youth can offer a buffer against grief's paralyzing effects while the vulnerabilities of age can intensify the experience.

Grief alone is debilitating. It zaps you of your life energy. I describe myself as feeling "paralyzed." I am sure if I had been older and in poor health, the grieving process would have been much different. I don't want to make comparisons using "better" or "worse," but the aging process and the interpersonal dynamic of spending the majority of your life with someone can cause significant emotional and physical health issues. It is not uncommon for an elderly spouse to die soon after their partner.

At the other end of the spectrum were my children. Vincent was school aged and had to deal with feeling different from his friends. Tori was three and unable to fully understand her dad would not be coming home. When I told her what had happened, she told me he was the strongest man in the world and would lift up the building. She started having difficulty sleeping. She also cried anytime I wanted to leave the house without her.

Although I believed Noah was incapable of understanding the loss and grieving at eighteen months old, my research has taught me otherwise. According to Child Development Specialist Rebecca Parlakian,

> Infants can experience grief, particularly when they are grieving a primary caregiver. This comes as a surprise to many adults, but imagine an infant—who is so dependent on caregivers to have their needs met, who is held by a caregiver, gazes into their caregiver's eyes, and knows this

caregiver's touch as they are fed, diapered, and bathed. This caregiver knows the infant and is able to provide comfort, reassurance, soothing. When the infant is unable to calm (researchers call this self-regulation), the caregiver uses herself to help the infant calm (through soothing touch, holding, soft words, swaying)—we call this co-regulation, and it's an important part of early relationship-building. And then, all of a sudden, this caregiver is gone.... The infant is distressed and protests the loss of his/her caregiver, may be irritable/hard to console, may cry more (while some babies may be more quiet or "shut down"), may appear to be searching for someone, may be less responsive/have a "flatter" expression, may seem anxious, and/or may be less hungry/ experience temporary weight loss.[7]

Children also have to deal with their loss over and over throughout their lives. Every milestone becomes bittersweet. Graduations, weddings, births, and everyday happenings— something will forever be missing. Addressing grief in children, and expecting to address it as they grow and mature and experience their loss at different developmental stages, is important. Naturally, seek professional help when necessary. Grief is never outgrown.

Spirituality and cultural identity can either hinder or facilitate the grieving process, highlighting the importance of aligning our healing with our deepest values. Individuals with stronger spiritual beliefs tend to navigate and resolve their grief more swiftly and comprehensively following the death of a loved one compared to those without spiritual beliefs.[8]

In certain cases, most often those involving sexual assault, our religious, spiritual, and cultural belief systems may hinder our healing by creating guilt and shame. Women who are raped may be seen as "unclean," fostering a soul-deep level of shame and self-hatred. In a study conducted on college-aged women, those who experienced rape were more likely to experience religious change compared to those who had not experienced rape and those who had experienced other traumas.

Rape not only related to significant changes in religiosity, but religiosity was shown to play a role in important elements of recovery: acknowledgment and disclosure. Sexism and rape myth acceptance significantly mediated the relationship between extrinsic religiosity and rape acknowledgment, and nonreligious individuals were less likely to disclose to their friends when they perceived them to be highly religious.[9]

This underscores the complex interplay between spirituality, cultural beliefs, and the aftermath of sexual assault, emphasizing the need for a nuanced understanding in supporting survivors. As individuals, it is also important for us to sift through our own value system to establish morals based on what feels most true to our soul. We can't simply buy into the narrative we were fed by our familial, religious, or cultural institutions. We must develop our own moral compass.

Community is the single most important tool for healing, and access to support and resources play a significant role in healing from any grief or trauma. I would not be where I am today without my family, friends, and even strangers who became pillars of strength. Having a lending ear or an extra set of hands makes the experience of loss much less scary and overwhelming.

We can find support in many places, but the key is being able to accept the support. You are worthy of it, and you need it! I vividly recall the shocking impact of my community during challenging times. Neighbors delivered meals while firefighters Jeff had worked with handled any home improvements. Friends dedicated countless hours to assist with whatever tasks needed attention. Jeff's best friend Danny would come over and help with the kids almost daily. We laugh about some of it now, like the time my daughter applied makeup to this large, towering man who then proceeded to leave, forgetting about his green eyeshadow, and went to the deli to buy something on the way home. He couldn't understand why everyone was looking at him like he was crazy until he saw himself in the mirror at home! My family was my lifeline. Saying, "Thank you," does not come close to expressing the gratitude I feel toward everyone who held me up during those awful days.

When it comes to resources, we need to be honest. It costs a lot of money to heal—whether that means burying a loved one or finding the right treatment for whatever caused your grief or trauma. The good news is there are many ways to get help through state and federal funds, community initiatives, and nonprofit organizations. These sources are meant to be utilized. Use them. Recently at a conference focused on supporting communities affected by mass violence, I learned funds are often designated specifically for these causes and often sit unused.

Some smaller but no less significant examples of support are apps, which are accessible to anyone who owns a smartphone. There are apps for everything—meditation, fitness, stress and time management, prayers and daily inspiration, even meal trains. It may take some time and energy to find what you're looking for, but it is worth it. We will speak more about resources and support in the chapter on community.

Recognizing the varied forms of grief is essential in validating and honoring all experiences of loss.

If you have experienced multiple losses, you may have a prolonged or complex grief experience, as explained above. What also holds true is that as we move through life and loss, we gain wisdom. We learn how to navigate tough experiences, and we know that when we move from our heart, we can survive and come out the other side. Previous loss can help increase our own personal level of resiliency—a valuable tool when we are in a place of suffering.

The nature of the relationship is pretty obvious when it comes to grief. Losing someone we care deeply about is much different than losing someone we don't have a close relationship with. What many do not consider is disenfranchised grief. Disenfranchised grief, as defined by Ken Doka, is pain that results when a person experiences a significant loss, and the resultant grief is not openly acknowledged, socially validated, or publicly mourned. In short, although the individual is experiencing a grief reaction, there is no social recognition the person has a right to grieve or a claim for social sympathy or support.[10] Examples of disenfranchised grief include perinatal loss such as miscarriage, loss of significant others when not married, death of a loved one due to overdose or suicide, unacknowledged children when a parent dies, and loss of a pet.

When I was working as a registered nurse during the AIDS epidemic, I often saw partners denied visitation with their loved one because legally they were not next of kin. It was heartbreaking. Similarly, Gold Star widows who lost spouses to suicide often faced exclusion from events supporting loss in the military community because the deaths did not occur on the physical battlefield. The experience of disenfranchised grief leaves individuals feeling isolated and misunderstood. Lacking acknowledgment for their pain, they may grapple with finding healthy coping mechanisms, potentially leading to complications in the grieving process or prolonged distress on a psychological level.

The manner of loss, whether sudden and traumatic or anticipated, also shapes our journey through grief. Violent, unforeseen deaths that leave no room for goodbyes often result in traumatic grief. Examples of such traumatic losses abound. The loss of thousands of lives of those who simply went to work in the morning or got on a plane only to never return to their families is a textbook example of what causes traumatic grief; school shootings, both accidental and planned suicides, the ongoing impact of COVID-19, car accidents, the recent withdrawal from Afghanistan, and the pervasive war scenes depicted daily across various media outlets are others. Each of these instances can precipitate traumatic grief, adding an extra layer of complexity to the already challenging journey of bereavement.

If traumatic grief is caused by an untimely, unexpected death or loss, anticipatory grief is its opposite. Anticipatory grief is a state of deep, painful sorrow that occurs before an impending loss. It can affect people facing the imminent death of a loved one or their own death. The term can also be applied to a loss not associated with death, such as the anticipation of losing a breast during a mastectomy, of facing a looming divorce, or of being diagnosed with a progressive condition like Alzheimer's disease.[11] It is commonly seen in caregivers and those being cared for, often happening simultaneously.

I experienced this while waiting for news from Ground Zero. As time went on, the likelihood of Jeff being found alive dwindled. All I could do was hold on to hope. With conventional grief, your emotions and actions are reactive. With anticipatory grief, your emotions and actions are largely proactive.[12] This type of grief can lead to a sense of detachment as we distance ourselves from loved ones as a means of coping. Anticipatory grief can bring feelings of guilt and shame, but it can also help someone sort through their emotions. It is a natural response to the awareness of impending loss. Cancer, chronic illness, and neurological diseases, such as Alzheimer's and dementia, may create anticipatory grief. To cope with anticipatory grief, it is important to share your feelings, maintain a reasonable amount of hope, and to also plan for your loss.

If there is a lack of closure, no physical body to accompany the loss, or no mourning ritual, as is the case in kidnappings, disappearances, POWs and many victims of 9/11, there may be an experience of ambiguous loss. They are unresolved scenarios, and the death is unclear or not confirmed. An article in the *New York Times Magazine* describes these as losses without "conclusion," in the traditional sense of the term, an experience of paradox—a simultaneous absence and presence—that eluded resolution.[13]

The words "unaccounted for" haunted me for weeks after the towers fell. Exactly forty days after the attack, Jeff's remains were recovered. Sadly, even after two decades, some families remain without closure, lacking any proof of their loved ones' fate on that tragic day. The advances in DNA identification offer hope for resolution, a prayer for those still waiting. Reflecting on this, I imagine victims of crime enduring a similar ambiguous grief when justice is elusive or punitive measures fall short. Coping with such loss is a formidable challenge, as our minds instinctively delve into denial to shield us from the pain. Seeking professional help or joining a support group becomes crucial in navigating the complexities of ambiguous loss.

While grief is an inevitable universal experience, the journey through it is deeply individual, marked by the interplay of personal experiences, cultural influences, emotional strength, and the specific nature of our losses. Recognizing the diverse factors that shape our grieving process sheds light on the path to healing, highlighting the idea that although the experience of loss is universal, our paths through it are uniquely our own. By acknowledging the complexity of grief, we grant ourselves the grace to heal on our own terms, finding comfort in the shared human experiences of love, loss, and the possibility of renewal.

CHAPTER 7

Pain Is a Privilege

In 2016, I committed to a sixty-mile hike over Memorial Day Weekend, a tribute to the fallen. We would hike from Harpers Ferry, West Virginia, to Section 60 in Arlington Cemetery carrying everything we needed to survive the next three days in a backpack that weighed close to thirty-five pounds. The first few miles were a grueling uphill hike on the Appalachian Trail.

"Pain is a privilege." I wish I could take credit for this quote. I have heard it countless times over the past two decades, and its impact has never lessened. These four simple words took me over a decade to embrace. That weekend, I learned the power of pain.

The breathtaking scenery of the Appalachian Trail was lost in my struggle to keep up with my team. After the first twenty or so miles, my feet had blistered. Every step felt like I was walking on shards of glass. I hadn't ever experienced anything so uncomfortable. I was relying on the support of my teammates.

One teammate, Ski, the person who had brought me to this event, carried my ruck for a while when my legs began to cramp from dehydration. Our team leader, Tony, with his southern twang, kept tabs on me when I became quiet. Another teammate, Kevin, who in future years would become my team leader and a trusted friend, kept me distracted with his sense of humor. Still, the idea of having to go another forty miles was daunting.

Every couple of miles we would stop to grab a snack, check our feet, pee in the woods, and, most importantly, share the heroic stories of fallen service members. It was a hot day. I was drinking water but not nearly enough. I was the newbie. I felt ashamed to have to ask for help or to make the ruck harder by slowing down my team. I was completely out of my comfort zone. I would replay the names of those I knew from the military and 9/11, visualizing what they had endured even though I truly had no idea. It became a mental struggle. I learned that your mind will quit way before your body.

I made it down the mountain. I counted that as my first win. We ended the first day at a local firehouse where we were fed our only substantial meal of the day. We slept outside on a grassy knoll in a sleeping bag—no tents allowed. I was not prepared for the swelling and pain that would come once we stopped moving. I was also not prepared for the spiders crawling all over us. I pulled myself as far into my sleeping bag as I could go. We were stepping off by 4:30 a.m. My mind was so filled with fear of failure that I barely slept.

I was up early to tape and wrap my feet. Miraculously, no other part of my body hurt. The following day we reached the halfway mark. It was a long stop at a local brewery. Here I was given the opportunity to share my "Story of Valor," as did a few other teammates. That first year, I had rucked in honor of USMC First Lieutenant Robert Kelly, who was assigned to 3rd Battalion/5th Marines when he was killed in action by an improvised explosive device on November 9, 2010, while deployed to Sangin, Afghanistan, during Operation Enduring Freedom. He took up the flag, the promise to defend the people of our country, that my husband had handed off. His sister, Kate, and her husband Jake met me at that brewery.

We shared a moment I will never forget. I asked Kate to join me on the stage and read the letter she entrusted to me that she had written about her beloved brother. She wanted to choke me initially because this wasn't planned at all. Depicting how Robert lived was so much more impactful than focusing on how he died. We said his name. So did every person in that room. Kate was so brave in that moment. It inspired me.

Kate and I met through our mutual friend, Tina Atherall. Our shared stories of loss created an unspoken connection. Hearing the pride and longing in Kate's voice as she retold stories of Robert reminded me our loved ones live on through our actions. We carry their legacy by storytelling, by always saying their names, and never allowing their sacrifice to be forgotten. It was pivotal in my mental state. I was determined to complete this mission of carrying his memory alongside my husband's and all the others who had willingly chosen to lay down their lives for the good of others.

The break at the brewery was coming to an end. At this point, I got a good look at my chewed-up feet. Barely a spot was left unblistered. I learned quickly the value of proper foot care during a ruck. Jake, Kate's husband, a Marine who had lost his leg in combat and was no stranger to rucking and wound care, helped to wrap my feet. He later shared with Kate that he would be surprised if I could finish with my feet in that condition.

I had to make a conscious choice to accept the pain. If I didn't, I would never finish. I told myself this pain was temporary and nothing like the pain I felt when Jeff died. My "why" echoed through my mind: the image of my husband scaling countless flights of stairs amid chaos, directing others to head in the opposite direction to safety; my children who transformed loss into motivation rather than a crutch. It encompassed the brave men and women defending our country, enduring austere conditions and harsh injuries— many never returning home, sacrificing their lives for a cause greater than themselves.

Those who did return were fighting demons only they could see. The Kellys and other families I had a personal connection with, their loved ones resting in Arlington and other national cemeteries, added weight to my resolve. The rest of the day, we made our way along miles of hard, unforgiving blacktop. As long as we kept moving, I was fine. The stopping and starting was excruciating.

I resorted to literally focusing on one foot in front of the other. Right, left, right, left. I could always take one more step. I had lost any appetite, but I forced myself to eat something small every hour because my body needed nourishment.

The second night was pitch black as we made our way along the W&OD trail. All I could see was the ChemLight of the person in front of me. I felt as if I was sleepwalking. I may have even dozed off while on my feet. I'd never done that before. I would put my headphones in and get lost in the emotions of songs.

I had periods of remembering different events in my life, but they came to me from a new perspective—times I took for granted because they were so simple, unimportant events I had wasted so much energy on. I was learning firsthand what fighting demons meant.

Demons are those parts of ourselves we sometimes regret and place into a box where we can easily ignore them. It may be the shameful memories of times when we didn't show up as the most stellar versions or ourselves or where we mistook the extraordinary for the ordinary. Those final sweet kisses goodbye, the shared private jokes, unspoken words left sitting in our hearts—they all came out to play in the cover of darkness.

The second night, we slept on concrete under the shadow of the Iwo Jima Memorial. I slept on a pizza box with my legs up against a stone wall to help with swelling and pain. The final day was our shortest day. Only eight miles out of sixty to complete. I was almost there. When the time came to get up and go, I was so sleep deprived and in so much pain that I didn't believe I could finish the final movement.

I went to Tony, my team leader, and told him how I felt. He was not having it. He believed in me more than I believed in myself. Being an Army Ranger, he was intolerant of quitting. He was also well-versed in the power of the human spirit. Definitely not his first time at this rodeo, he told me in a stern voice to take some Advil and to ruck up, and I would be fine. *Ugh.* I trusted him. I followed his orders. I was also planning on meeting Kate at her brother's grave once we reached Arlington.

In the depths of the urge to quit, a revelation emerged— the pain was a privilege. This may sound paradoxical at first. It may even seem offensive to those who, through no fault of their own, seem to exist in a constant state of pain. The challenges and hardships we endure often force us to develop coping mechanisms, strength, and adaptability that we might not have otherwise discovered within ourselves. It can deepen our empathy and understanding for others who are suffering. This can lead to stronger connections with others and a greater capacity to offer support and compassion. Experiencing pain can make the moments of joy and happiness much sweeter. Knowing what it's like to suffer can make the good times feel more precious and can teach us not to take the positive aspects of our lives for granted. It can serve as a catalyst for reevaluating life choices, changing direction, or finding new meaning and purpose in life.

That final push was through the war memorials located in the National Mall in Washington, DC, our nation's capital. Led by bagpipers, we walked silently through each one in rows of two or single file. We observed families, teammates, and brothers lining up to honor those who gave their lives in service to our country. World War I, World War II, the endless number of names listed on the shadowy Vietnam Memorial.

We walked over the Memorial Bridge, carrying the colors of each branch of our United States Armed Forces. People stopped and saluted. They honked their horns. The kids waved. It was something to behold. I was hobbling, but damn I was proud and humbled.

We arrived at Arlington. Hugs and coins were handed out as our event came to an end. I wasn't finished yet. I wanted to visit Section 60. Kate had called and said traffic was impossible. She probably wouldn't make it on time. I was resolute in making it to Robert's grave. It was much further than I expected, but I had come this far. I was not leaving without seeing it. As I approached, I saw people there. It was Kate's mother and father visiting their son.

I could barely walk and hadn't showered in three days. Instantly, I forgot about all of that as I was overcome with emotion. I feel like I fell into Mrs. Kelly's arms. I was sobbing. All the emotions that had surfaced over the past three days found their way out through my tears. It was one of the few times I cried without hesitation. The Kellys were incredibly kind and very appreciative that we had honored Robert. It made every step worth it.

I finished that hike, and in doing so I learned my mind will always look for the place of most comfort. Comfort often becomes a place of complacency—a place of forgetting and the place where the easier option is quitting. Comfort is not always the place we grow but the place where we sink back into the familiar. Familiar does not equal healthy. Familiar is often the chaos we are used to, the generational trauma, the learned behaviors. Familiar comfort is the place where our growth is stunted, or worse, where we wither away.

The choice between the familiar and the uncomfortable is the choice we have the privilege of making. Never underestimate the power of taking yourself out of your comfort zone. Pain became more than a challenge; it evolved into an opportunity to elevate my resilience. I had successfully widened my window of tolerance physically, mentally, and spiritually.

Viewing pain as a privilege does not diminish its difficulty or the suffering it causes. Instead, it acknowledges that within the heart of suffering lie valuable lessons and opportunities for growth that can lead to a richer experience of life.

■

CHAPTER 8

Courage and Your Comfort Zone

Grief has often been said to be the price we pay, or penalty, for having loved. The word pain is derived from the Latin word "poena"—meaning penalty. We live in a society that avoids pain and discomfort at all costs. If you don't believe me, read the stats on opioid addiction or alcoholism. According to the Centers for Disease Control and Prevention (CDC), more than eighty thousand drug overdose deaths in the United States in 2021 involved opioids. This number is a significant increase from the previous year, with a 30 percent rise in opioid overdose deaths from 2019 to 2022. Synthetic opioids, such as fentanyl, were involved in nearly 88 percent of these deaths.[1]

Additionally, the prevalence of alcohol use disorder (AUD) highlights our collective struggle with discomfort. According to statistics, one in ten Americans over the age of twelve grapples with AUD.[2] AUD is clinically defined as a chronic medical condition, where individuals find themselves unable to control or cease alcohol consumption despite adverse consequences.[3] We are all searching for ways to avoid being uncomfortable. Avoiding pain is instinctually built into our DNA. Avoidance of pain is the main job of our central nervous system.

Pain exists on various levels—the physical, the mental, the emotional, and the spiritual. Not only do they coexist with one another, but they shapeshift from one into another. These levels are intricately interwoven, capable of transforming seamlessly from one form to another. The emotional pain manifests into physical illness and vice versa. The question then arises: How can pain, in all its multifaceted complexity, ever be deemed a privilege?

To answer this question effectively, we must understand the complex workings of our brain and body in response to trauma and grief. Next, it's crucial to grasp the dynamic interplay between the brain, the body, and the emotional mind. Finally, we must acknowledge and make space for what I refer to as our soul—the intrinsic and untouchable core of our being. Grief, trauma, and loss are not the same, but they are inherently connected. Grief can occur without trauma, trauma does not happen without grief, and loss is the common thread woven into both experiences.

Bessel van der Kolk, a prominent psychiatrist and trauma researcher who authored *The Body Keeps the Score: Brain, Mind, and Body in the Healing of Trauma*, defines trauma as "an event or a series of events that overwhelms an individual's capacity to cope, disrupts their sense of safety, and leaves imprints on their body, brain, and mind."[4] He emphasizes that trauma is not solely defined by the event itself but by the individual's subjective experience and the resulting impact on their psychological and physiological well-being. Van der Kolk highlights the importance of understanding trauma as a whole-body experience.

Gabor Maté, a renowned physician, addiction expert, and author, has a similar definition of trauma. He states trauma is "any event or set of circumstances that is experienced by an individual as physically or emotionally harmful or life-threatening and that has lasting adverse effects on the individual's functioning and mental, physical, social, emotional, or spiritual well-being."[5] He says, very simply, the event is what happens on the outside, and trauma is what happens on the inside. As you can see, both experts agree that trauma exerts its impact across every facet of our existence.

The most visible effects of trauma can be seen through our bodies. When faced with a traumatic event, the initial reaction engages the most ancient and instinctual segment of our brain—the limbic system. Comprising components like the amygdala, hippocampus, thalamus, hypothalamus, basal ganglia, and cingulate gyrus, the limbic system governs emotions and memories, orchestrating automatic responses to emotional stimuli.

Because the limbic system is one of the oldest parts of our brains in evolutionary terms, most writers and professors will use the example of being attacked by a lion because it demonstrates the threats our ancestors had to face. In this scenario, we envision a very primal human wandering through a tree-dense area when they are startled by the appearance of a lion. The brain swiftly recognizes a threat, prompting the amygdala to activate and initiate fear responses, leading to the release of stress hormones such as cortisol and adrenaline. These hormones prepare the body to either confront the threat or escape from it.

The orchestration of physiological changes is intricate: the heart rate escalates, propelling more blood to muscles and vital organs, priming the body for action. Pupils dilate, amplifying vision and focus by allowing more light to enter. Breathing intensifies, delivering a surge of oxygen to muscles and the brain, optimizing overall performance. Elevated blood pressure expedites the transport of oxygen and nutrients to organs and muscles, redirecting blood flow away from nonessential systems like digestion and resulting in a slowdown. Sweating increases, regulating body temperature during exertion. Senses heighten and sharpen, enhancing our ability to assess potential threats. Blood sugar levels spike, providing the body with extra energy for immediate demands. Notably, the immune system temporarily deactivates, prioritizing immediate survival responses over long-term protection.

This coordinated physiological response is commonly known as the fight-or-flight reaction. Now you know why your palms become sweaty, your heart races, and your breathing changes when you feel nervous or scared.

If that sounds as if your body is a brilliantly engineered machine, you're right! We are hardwired to survive. Even more amazing is that this isn't the only thing happening. At the same time, the prefrontal cortex, which is responsible for decision-making, impulse control, and emotional regulation, becomes less active.

We are now operating on instinct alone. This is very animalistic in nature. The ability for a person to think clearly, make rational decisions, and regulate emotions is impaired. The person only has the ability to react through pure gut feeling. All of the physical changes allow that reaction to happen without any logical choice.

Broca's area, situated within the prefrontal cortex, plays a pivotal role in the articulation of speech and is often affected by traumatic experiences. This can shed light on the common phenomenon where, in moments of fear, individuals find themselves at a loss for words. Additionally, this impact on Broca's area contributes to the difficulty many experience in expressing their traumatic or painful experiences in words.

Another noteworthy change in brain activity is the alteration of the hippocampus, the brain region involved in memory formation and consolidation, leading to difficulty in memory processing and retrieval. This, in turn, impacts our cognition, resulting in fragmented or incomplete memories of the traumatic event and difficulty distinguishing between past and present experiences. In other words, we often can only recall snapshots of traumatic events, as I stated in the introduction of the book.

This also explains why we can be triggered by much smaller nonthreatening events in our lives after experiencing a major traumatic event. Our brain loses the capacity to determine what has happened in the past versus what is actually happening in the present, and we are put right back into the stress response cycle. Remember, the brain desires to protect us, but sometimes the inability to distinguish between a true threat and a perceived threat can do more harm than good. For a deeper dive into the neurobiology of trauma, please check out *The Body Keeps the Score: Brain, Mind, and Body in the Healing of Trauma* by Bessel van der Kolk.

Regardless of its adverse effects, the fight-or-flight response is a normal, healthy, and acute response that improves our chances of survival in dangerous situations. It means that once the lion wanders off in the other direction without eating us alive, our nervous system returns to a regulated state. A chronic activation of the stress response and dysregulation of the nervous system is what we know as PTSD, which we will discuss more in depth later in this book.

Two lesser-known distinct reactions to perceived threats and dangerous situations are fawn and freeze responses. These responses are triggered when we aren't able to fight or escape our threat. The fawn response is a survival instinct where an individual tends to try to appease or please the threat to ensure their safety. An example of this would be negotiating or complying with an assailant to avoid further harm ("I won't tell anyone, please let me go"), or an abused wife doting over her abuser.

The freeze response is a reaction of immobilization, or "playing dead," in the face of the threat. This freeze response is often dissociation of the attacked, feeling as if they have left their body and are an outside observer. Freeze is commonly seen in instances where there is no ability to escape. The entire body shuts down, frozen in fear. This is not a consciously controlled response. Freeze response often occurs in children, instances of severe physical harm or torture, and in victims of sexual assault.

While fawn and freeze responses are adaptive and can increase our ability to survive, if they persist in nonthreatening situations, they can become maladaptive and hinder a person's ability to protect themselves. When dissociation or freezing becomes the brain's "go-to" coping mechanism out of familiarity, it will resort to that when the better option is to remove oneself from the present situation.

In addition to the physical alterations that trauma brings about, it also deeply influences our mental landscape, shaping our thoughts, feelings, and behaviors. After a traumatic event, people often describe having intrusive thoughts. These thoughts usually center around memories or images of the event. Intrusive thoughts can make concentrating and completing daily tasks extremely difficult. Emotional dysregulation also occurs. Heightened anxiety, fear, anger, sadness, or even emotional numbness can become challenging to regulate or express effectively.

Hypervigilance and hyperarousal are often developed in trauma survivors. They will find themselves constantly scanning for potential threats. This commonly leads to insomnia, lack of concentration, and an increased startle response. The mind is on constant alert.

Avoidance and numbing are two more emotional responses. The traumatized individual will avoid reminders of the event or numb their emotions. Lastly, trauma adversely impacts memory by creating gaps or inaccuracies in recall and decreasing cognition, causing the phenomenon of "magical thinking" coined by Joan Didion.

What makes something traumatic is the person's reaction to any particular event, not the event itself. What I experience as trauma may not be traumatic to you or someone else. One thing clear with trauma is that a loss of some sort is involved. Whenever we lose something that matters in our lives, we experience grief. This is why the two are enmeshed.

All of this stuff sounds very scientific and also *very* shitty! Who would ever consider this a privilege?

Rumi, the thirteenth-century Persian poet, once penned, "The wound is where the light enters," encapsulating a profound privilege bestowed upon those who endure profound suffering. Contemplating this and similar quotes, I envision a dark room, perhaps even a prison cell, stripped of all light—a cold and unforgiving space. Then someone opens the door just a crack, and behold, the light pours in. Even the tiniest gleam can initially blind us until our eyes adjust. Once we can see, clarity reigns. No stumbling, no fear—we discern our surroundings. Everything hidden in the darkness becomes visible in the light.

Pain, then, becomes the chance to shine a metaphorical light on every facet of our being. I know for some this sounds New Age and a bit freaky, but listen up. A reason these clichés and quotes last for centuries is simply because they are true and timeless. Humanity has weathered famine, poverty, enslavement, war, disease, and loneliness throughout history. Pain, trauma, loss, grief—all experiences we'd prefer to avoid. Yet due to the fact we live in a society fixated on its problems, we often overlook what awaits on the other side of pain: *growth*.

For many people, the only time we reevaluate who we are and how we show up in this world is when we are forced to be uncomfortable. Pain is a symptom of a larger problem. It is our internal emergency broadcast system alerting us to pay attention. When grief engulfs us, many of us become quite creative in how we try to numb away this pain. Some of us get drunk, some work out like crazy, and some lie around doing nothing at all until, as I love to say, "we get sick of our own shit."

Important side note about pain: As humans we are only able to experience one type of pain at a time. By experiencing physical pain, we override mental and emotional pain. This is why people may attempt to cope through cutting, pulling out their own hair, taking part in extreme physical activities, and the like.

However, when we find ourselves trapped in the cycles of numbing, dissociation, or avoidance, the door to growth slowly closes. Pain points us to the areas within us that are begging for attention, pleading for us to take a closer look. When we are courageous enough to sit with the pain grief and trauma create, it is as if we are opening the door to let the light in.

Feeling is a privilege reserved for those of us blessed with these human bodies. When we numb the pain, we numb the joy. In the military, there is a phrase: "Embrace the suck." It implies facing hardships or discomfort head-on, acknowledging the difficulty but choosing to persevere and find strength or growth in the midst of adversity. As we become more adept at addressing our pain, we also become more adept at recognizing and experiencing joy and happiness.

Some individuals postpone seeking solutions until the discomfort becomes unbearable—when the numbness and dissociation leave them feeling even emptier than the grief and trauma they were attempting to shield themselves from. It often involves a journey of trial and error to discover healthy ways to soothe pain and reconnect with the soul—the part of ourselves that remains perpetually whole.

I need to stress the *courage* it takes to look at all the parts of ourselves lingering in the shadows. The little girl who was told she wasn't good enough. The little boy who was shamed into thinking he would never amount to anything. The woman who feels as if she will never be able to sleep peacefully again. The veteran who took the life of a child being held up as a human shield. The pieces of ourselves that we are ashamed of, that we struggle to keep hidden from ourselves and those around us. We all have these dark corners where pain hides. In the effort, the forward movement, the gathering of information, the self-reflection and application of all we learn, healing is created. When we shine the light, we realize these places aren't so bad at all. They are misunderstood. Grief and trauma prey on these versions of ourselves.

There is no "one size fits all" recipe for healing from devastating loss. But one thing is for sure—you have to feel it to heal it. The healing process is strengthening. It creates resilience. I remember when my son broke his clavicle. He was a high school baseball player on his way to becoming a Division 1 catcher. I was nervous for his return behind the plate because we are taught when something breaks it's weakened. I could vividly see in my mind the commonplace collision at home causing further injury. Imagine my surprise and relief when the doctor told me the calcium that had formed around the break actually makes the bone stronger than before. This is the beauty of being human. Our so-called "brokenness," when healed properly, can become our greatest strengths.

CHAPTER 9

Breaking Chains

The term "trauma" originates from a Greek word that translates to "wound," "shock," or "injury." When we talk about psychological trauma, we refer to the emotional turmoil a person endures in response to an event—or series of events—that far exceeds their ability to cope or make sense of the emotions involved. Such events, whether singular or recurrent, are perceived as intensely damaging or even life-threatening to oneself or those close to the individual.

It's crucial to recognize that people vary significantly in how they internalize and respond to experiences. Consequently, an event that profoundly affects one person might not have the same emotional impact on another. Bessel van der Kolk, in his revered book *The Body Keeps the Score: Brain, Mind, and Body in the Healing of Trauma*, states that trauma, by definition, is unbearable and intolerable.[1]

Traumatic experiences undermine a person's sense of safety in the world and create a sense that catastrophe could strike at any time. Parental loss in childhood, motor vehicle accidents, physical violence, sexual assault, military combat experiences, earthquakes, the unexpected loss of a loved one—any sudden, violent disruption—are events that can lead to trauma. People typically replay the experience in their mind over and over and ruminate on what happened. The experience leads to changes in brain function.[2] Children are particularly susceptible to trauma due to their lack of control over their environments.

Based on a survey of nearly sixty-nine thousand adults in twenty-four countries, the World Mental Health Survey Consortium found that 70 percent of adults have had at least one experience of trauma in their life.[3] Although subjective, trauma is a relatively universal experience. Most people who experience trauma will recover in a healthy manner over time. It is estimated that only 3 percent to 10 percent of people who undergo a traumatic experience have persistent mental health difficulties known as post-traumatic stress disorder (PTSD). In simplest terms, PTSD is when a past trauma continues to play out in your present life. Van der Kolk would argue that trauma is physically seared into the nervous system, more like a scar than a story. If it was true, it would mean trauma could act as a kind of objective proof that something had happened. A person can lie, but the body cannot.[4]

My reaction to the phone ringing during my acupuncture session—being physically jolted back to the moment I first learned of the World Trade Center attack—was a manifestation of post-traumatic stress.

I was recently diagnosed with complex PTSD (C-PTSD). Just for clarity's sake, C-PTSD is a psychological condition that can develop after prolonged trauma, often involving interpersonal relationships. It is not yet recognized as a separate diagnosis in the DSM-5, but it hopefully will be in the newest edition. C-PTSD is most commonly associated with childhood abuse, domestic violence, war, or long-term captivity. The symptoms are similar to PTSD but can be more complex and long-lasting. They include emotional dysregulation; distorted self-perception with feelings of shame, guilt, and low self-esteem; problems trusting, forming, and maintaining relationships; physical symptoms such as headache or GI problems without a clear medical cause; and dissociation.

Experiencing multiple traumatic events in your life colors your response to trauma and grief. It may even go so far as to play a role in your day-to-day life. I had a childhood riddled with trauma. My biological father left when I was two. My family had a history of domestic violence, abuse, and addiction for generations. My first marriage, which lasted only a year, ended because my ex-husband became an abusive addict. I had perpetuated the dysfunction that was familiar to me because I thought this was acceptable. This is only the tip of the iceberg, but you get the idea.

Before I sought help after Jeff died, I saw myself as a strong and resilient woman who had overcome many hardships. This is certainly true. The problem was I had not integrated any of the trauma. I had simply survived by using skills I had acquired in childhood such as dissociation, self-blame, substance abuse in the form of cigarettes and alcohol, avoidance, aggression, emotional numbing, and hypervigilance.

All of this had been modeled for me in different relationships, and I employed them throughout different periods of my life. My nervous system had been imprinted, and it was utilizing whatever tools it had at the time. I hadn't ever discussed the trauma I experienced because I grew up in a culture that stressed: "What goes on in our home stays in our home."

Does that sound familiar to you? This creates even further shame. Not talking, not sharing trauma, means certain death for our hearts and souls.[5] The other reason I hadn't sought help was because I didn't know how dysfunctional this way of living was. It was all I had known for many years. These tools were neither healing nor sustainable.

I have witnessed firsthand these same behaviors in almost all of the service members I have had the honor of working with. Most have a history of trauma prior to entering the military. I have seen it in my own first responder community. I have seen it in friends who have suffered losses. We all see it in our larger community after COVID-19 lockdowns. Did anyone else find it interesting that liquor stores were deemed an essential business? When we do not have the proper tools, we all resort to our default settings. These settings are determined in childhood or have been engrained from various other traumas. Previous trauma experiences set the tone for our grieving process.

If this all sounds depressing to you, take heart! This space is the same space where the magic happens. When I realized my unhealthy coping skills were not working, I searched for something different. This search made me realize I had a *choice*. No, I did not have a choice in my husband dying and leaving me alone at thirty-two with three young children to raise. No, you didn't have a choice when you were assaulted. You didn't have a choice on the battlefield when you had to defend your life and the lives of those next to you. *But*, and this is a *huge* but... *you have a choice in how this will play out in the rest of your life.*

Most of us cannot do this work of unraveling years of unhealthy and unproductive coping skills alone. Seeking professional help was the best choice I ever made. To be quite frank, when I first decided to look for a therapist, it was not because I was sick of my own shit yet. It was out of fear of fucking up my children for the rest of their lives if I didn't do this right. I had no idea where to begin.

The woman who prided herself in being able to handle anything went out of her comfort zone and actively chose to look for help. Lucky for me, I found a therapist who knew true healing meant working through old wounds and addressing them with mind, body, and soul. She knew talking was helpful but not enough.

Jeff's death brought me to Mariann, and working with her brought me to myself. She held my hand as I walked through the graveyard of all the people I had been: The scared and lonely little girl who felt she had to protect everyone. The eleven-year-old who lost her grandmother, the person she loved the most and was so traumatized already that she couldn't even cry. The rebellious teenager who had no idea of her own self-worth. The scared pregnant nursing student who was determined to have a career and never be dependent upon anyone. The young mom who refused to let her son grow up in an unhealthy environment so she left with the clothes on her back and anything she could pack and carry to escape an abuser. The grieving widow who felt so broken that she wished it had been her in the towers instead of her husband. All the parts of me that I hid in shame and guilt and self-loathing. Mariann taught me these were my places of greatest strength if I could own them, accept them, and integrate them into my everyday life. This was the portal.

It started with self-awareness. I was taught how to be an observer of myself: notice my patterns of behavior, notice the outcomes. It was important to do this without judgment. I sucked at that part, but it got easier the more I practiced. If I didn't like the outcome, the next time I was in the same situation, I should choose differently. She encouraged me to pay attention to my body. Notice how it reacted in certain circumstances. When a family member was aggressive and I felt myself contract or fear and anger rise up in my belly, I was able to identify many other times in my life when my body had felt the same way. Now, rather than ignore it, I could listen and heed its warning to move to a place of safety, speak my mind, or remove myself completely. I had choices. I was no longer a powerless child.

This newfound self-awareness allowed me to become familiar with my own nervous system. In the example of the phone call, my body reacted out of imprinted memories. The sound of the phone created a cascade of neurotransmitters and hormones that caused my body to activate the sympathetic nervous system, which is the body's gas pedal. It prepares us to react to danger. Knowing that there was no danger at hand, I now had the tools to actively encourage my parasympathetic nervous system, my body's brake, to kick in. I could intentionally bring myself back to a feeling of safety. The GRACE model will offer insight into these tools.

Taking this journey is like reclaiming your own power. Imagine being able to heal every part of yourself and then putting all those pieces back together, only to find they've come back stronger, safer, and more vibrant than ever. As you show up for yourself, you learn to trust yourself. You essentially become the hero you needed at various points in your life—be it as a kid, a teen, or at any moment when a helping hand, a bit of guidance, or just some unconditional love would've made all the difference! I know this is easy to say but extremely hard to do. I was in therapy for many years after Jeff died, and I live a life of constant self-awareness and reflection. Recently, I made the choice to go back to therapy following the phone-ringing trigger. This isn't a linear journey. It is a constant evolution. The key take away is: Healing is a choice you have to make. It takes time, but time is *not* what heals, contrary to popular belief. Choosing yourself and your highest good in each moment heals.

Working through my own PTSD gave me more insight into the unhealthy behaviors that dominated both my immediate and extended families. I was then able to create healthy boundaries along with developing a healthier parenting style. The effects are evident in my now-grown children who are happy, healthy, and thriving. I couldn't be more grateful or feel more blessed.

When we heal our own trauma, we heal the generational trauma that has been handed down in our families, and we contribute to the healing of the collective.

CHAPTER 10

From Trauma to Transformation

PTSD (post-traumatic stress disorder) and traumatic grief share a common foundation in that both are responses to experiencing or witnessing traumatic events. However, they manifest differently and focus on separate aspects of the trauma experience.

PTSD is a mental health condition triggered by experiencing or witnessing a terrifying event, characterized by symptoms such as flashbacks, severe anxiety, nightmares, and uncontrollable thoughts about the event. It can result from a variety of traumatic incidents, including accidents, natural disasters, or violence. Although the words "trauma" and "PTSD" are used interchangeably, they are not the same. Experiencing trauma without experiencing PTSD is possible.

Women are more likely to develop PTSD than men. About eight of every one hundred women (or 8 percent) and four of every one hundred men (or 4 percent) will have PTSD at some point in their life. This is in part due to the types of traumatic events women are more likely to experience—such as sexual assault—compared to men. Veterans are more likely to have PTSD than civilians. Veterans who deployed to a war zone are also more likely to have PTSD than those who did not deploy.[1]

Traumatic grief, on the other hand, specifically relates to the intense and prolonged mourning that follows a death perceived as traumatic. This might involve the sudden, unexpected, or violent death of a loved one. While grief is a natural response to loss, traumatic grief encompasses a more complex reaction, where the individual struggles with accepting the loss due to the traumatic circumstances surrounding it.

The relation between PTSD and traumatic grief lies in their origins in trauma and the intense emotional distress they cause. Both can significantly impact an individual's functioning and quality of life. However, they require different approaches in treatment, with PTSD focusing on addressing the trauma itself and its psychological effects and traumatic grief concentrating on the processing of the loss and the complex emotions tied to it.

An individual can experience both PTSD and traumatic grief simultaneously, especially if the traumatic event involved the loss of a loved one. In such cases, integrated treatment approaches that address both the traumatic aspects of the event and the grief associated with the loss may be necessary.

Interestingly, the events of 9/11 identified trauma as a national health crisis, which brought about research and increased awareness around "trauma informed" treatment.

Similarly, COVID-19 held the spotlight to grief, allowing for acknowledgment and support.

The GRACE model has been a cornerstone in navigating my journey through PTSD and traumatic loss, touching on every aspect I found pivotal for healing. My confidence in its transformative power extends beyond my personal experience, having witnessed its radical impact across diverse groups. From veterans and those in recovery to healthcare professionals and caregivers, the model's reach and potency in addressing the deep-seated effects of trauma and loss are evident. Its success across such varied communities reinforces my belief in its potential to foster healing, resilience, and growth in the face of life's most challenging experiences.

PART II

G.R.A.C.E.

CHAPTER 11

G.R.A.C.E. Defined

We have dedicated considerable time to examining the impact of suffering. Diving into the depths of how loss and trauma fundamentally transform us, we've explored the profound shifts within ourselves. Now, it is time to revisit a core conviction of mine: Navigating through grief and trauma can serve as a gateway to unveiling our most authentic selves. In this spirit, I aim to introduce and elaborate on the key strategies I consider instrumental in forging the passage to the transformative gateway we seek.

In the past, I pitied people who had survived traumatic events or were devastated by loss. I felt like they could never recover and would never be the same. This perception was partly accurate. They indeed could never revert to their former selves. I was naive and wrong to believe they couldn't recover, though. My personal journey through adversity taught me that healing is not only possible, but it is also an opportunity for exponential growth. When I was hired to initiate a yoga program for an inpatient military wellness unit in the now defunct Holliswood Hospital, I witnessed a similar pattern of growth in service members who had been diagnosed with combat-related PTSD.

PTSD, or the pain of loss, doesn't have to be an endless cycle of pain, flashbacks, and rumination about the past. It can actually serve as an access point to transformation. The key is in choosing to step through this portal. At Holliswood, the service members often used the term "punching our demons in the throat," a powerful metaphor for confronting and overcoming their struggles. In the yoga sessions I led, I emphasized their reactions were not fixed traits but learned behaviors that could be unlearned. Much of this work is about creating a safe space to unravel long-held unexamined beliefs and behaviors that mask our true potential. This insight often sparked a flicker of hope within them.

Establishing a sense of safety within oneself is essential for neural rewiring, and yoga plays a crucial role in this process by helping to regulate the nervous system. Seeing one of these service members drift off to sleep during savasana, the concluding pose of a yoga session, was always a satisfying moment for me. Sometimes, it marked their first restful sleep in days, signaling a positive interaction with their nervous system.

Rewiring your nervous system, thanks to neuroplasticity, is like forging a path through a dense, untouched meadow. At first the trail is faint, but with persistent effort it becomes well-defined and easy to follow. Our brain always seeks the path of least resistance; therefore, it naturally prefers familiar, well-worn routes, often opting for them subconsciously. If those familiar paths are paved with the dysfunctional behaviors of our past, we can create new paths and behavior by responding differently. Metaphorically, we are choosing the path less traveled. When individuals commit to probing deeper, stepping out of their comfort zones, and embracing the healing process, we witness the phenomenon known as post-traumatic growth.

The concept of post-traumatic growth (PTG) was first developed in the middle of the 1990s while a more detailed model was only reached in recent years. PTG is defined as positive psychological changes experienced as a result of the struggle with trauma or highly challenging situations. This phenomenon should be considered not as an alternative but as a parallel process with respect to negative psychological consequences. PTG may feature positive changes in self-perception, interpersonal relationships, and philosophy of life, leading to increased self-awareness and self-confidence, a more open attitude toward others, a greater appreciation of life, and the discovering of new possibilities.[1]

The pivotal principal in post-traumatic growth is "choice." Facing a catastrophic loss or significant trauma often leaves us feeling powerless, stripped of any semblance of choice. While we may not have control over the traumatic events themselves, we retain the ultimate power to choose their impact on our future. This distinction is crucial, highlighting our agency in shaping the trajectory of our healing and growth. The victim mentality seems to have become quite common in our culture. The ultimate outcome of embracing the victim mentality is the stripping away of power to change your circumstance. We reclaim that power by choosing to take part in our own growth process.

We are the architects of our own meaning, shaping our existence through the decisions we make in response to life's challenges. This principle underscores the transformative power of embracing our agency, even in the darkest of times. You create the future with every choice you make and action you take.

I developed the acronym GRACE as a framework to encapsulate the essential components we can utilize when we choose to transmute our suffering into a force that empowers rather than devastates us. This model is designed to be applicable at both the community and individual levels. Recognizing the foundation of a resilient community lies in the resilience of its members. The premise is simple yet profound: Our collective well-being enhances when each individual thrives. GRACE serves as a roadmap, guiding us toward healing and strength while emphasizing that our shared journey toward growth not only uplifts ourselves but also strengthens everyone around us.

Grace is often described as a divine influence that works within humans to rejuvenate, inspire, and provide the fortitude to withstand trials. This resonates with me particularly because of its focus on divine intervention. As I mentioned earlier, research has indicated that the depth of one's spiritual beliefs can significantly influence how one copes with loss, underscoring the profound impact of spirituality on healing processes.[2]

This brings to mind an entertaining story about how the GRACE acronym was conceived. It felt as though the concept was channeled through me rather than a product of my own intellect. I simply sat down one day and effortlessly outlined the key components that had alchemized my own pain over two decades. I was initially content with the GRACE framework until I realized something was missing—my faith, which had been a cornerstone and compass throughout my journey.

Because I believed the acronym to have come from something higher than me, I couldn't imagine it being fallible. The challenge was incorporating "faith" without altering the existing letters. It wasn't about religion, per se, but something more sacred and comforting. Then it struck me: The essence of faith was already encapsulated in the word GRACE itself. Thank goodness! When I realized it was in front of me the entire time, it brought a sigh of relief and gratitude, affirming the completeness of the model.

The beauty of the GRACE model lies in its simplicity and memorability. It offers practical and accessible strategies for a wide audience, embodying a holistic approach to healing that integrates the transformative power of grace in both its spiritual and practical dimensions.

The tools offered in the GRACE model aren't written in any particular order of importance. In fact, healing is never linear. Rather, it resembles a series of concentric circles, continually guiding us inward to our core essence, our deepest truths, and our highest potential. We revisit our pain over and over.

These waves of grief wash over us at the most unexpected times. Each time we revisit it, we go a little deeper with our healing. The magic of this is that we aren't simply healing from the traumatic event. We are healing from anything and everything that has happened to us up until that point. Our past experiences shape, and sometimes dictate, our reactions, often stemming from unexamined, ingrained behaviors developed for protection rather than healing.

To illustrate, consider yet another personal story. I am the eldest of three siblings. I was responsible at a young age for helping to care for the younger children. I learned to be very independent—hyper-independent, actually. I never asked for help. I would rather poke myself in the eye with a pin. I was also easily annoyed by needy people. In the first few months after Jeff died, it was nearly impossible for me to function in a way that would be supportive and optimal for my children. I needed help. There was no doubt about that. I would never ask.

Fortunately, I had a robust support system and a therapist who encouraged me to seek help without guilt, especially for my children's sake. She told me that my only responsibility in those early times was to make sure they had what they needed, even if it meant asking someone else to provide it. Fortunately, my family was willing to step in and do just that on the days I could barely get out of bed. This marked a pivotal moment in my healing journey, allowing me to embrace the vulnerability of asking for help and affording myself the grace and space to heal not just in the present but also to address the deep-seated fears of my younger self. This process was transformative, highlighting the massive impact of giving ourselves permission to heal at all levels. Powerful shit. Life-changing shit.

On the surface, the steps I am about to name may seem simplistic and almost superficial, putting a Band-Aid on a bullet wound. In the following chapters, I will get into mechanisms of action and how each tool creates a change in our entire being—body, mind, and soul. Remember, we cannot completely heal without addressing all of who we are. The body does not work independently of the mind or the emotions. They all work simultaneously with one influencing the other. We don't heal one part of ourselves while neglecting another part.

The acronym GRACE stands for:

Gratitude

Radical acknowledgment

Action

Community

Emergent narrative

GRACE encompasses these tools.

They are the culmination of my journey, the basics I fall back to again and again. The foundation for the rebuilding of my most authentic self. You rely on these secret weapons when you choose to enter the portal that leads to your soul's purpose and highest self.

■

CHAPTER 12

Gratitude

In the fifty-five years I have walked this earth as an extremely flawed human, many things have saved my life, but none as profoundly as gratitude. In the past I might have attributed these moments to sheer luck. However, gratitude stands apart in its impact. Unlike the serendipitous nature of chance, gratitude is a deliberate practice, a conscious choice that has been foundational in saving me during my darkest hours.

I want to rewind back to the early days of my loss and set the scene for you. We had Jeff's memorial and buried the casket filled with items that symbolized who Jeff was. A few weeks later, his physical body was recovered from Ground Zero. We had a dedication for his remains at the cemetery.

For everyone else, this meant closure and moving on. I went from a home filled with people waiting on news and supporting my every need to deafening silence. Just me and my children. No distractions. No one to tend to the kids. No one doing my laundry. No one grocery shopping.

It all hit me like a runaway freight train. This was my life. I was responsible for everything. Overwhelmed was an understatement. Being bogged down with responsibility is one thing, but struggling with paralyzing traumatic grief is a whole other level. It was hard for me to get out bed. Every day I would open my eyes, and my first thought would be, *This has to be a nightmare. This can't be true. I don't want to face another minute of this anguish.*

These thoughts were immediately followed by my to-do list, which had grown dramatically because now *everything* was my job. *Get Vincent up and ready for school. Make his lunch. Throw in some laundry. Feed the babies. Get them dressed for the day. Do breakfast dishes. Run the vacuum. Fold the laundry. Make the beds. Hire someone to mow the lawn. The sink is dripping…* The list went on and on.

The idea of walking into this foreign life every day felt like a weight that was crushing me. Yet I needed to do it. I had no choice. At least, that was the way it felt at the time.

Night after night, I would find myself lying in my now-empty bed with my gaze fixed on the blank expanse of the ceiling, overwhelmed by the dread of the coming day. Each morning, the challenge was to find just one compelling reason to get up—to find that one spark of inspiration that would give me the energy to face my life. Often my only motivation was the thought of being one day closer to reuniting with Jeff. This marked the humble and pathetic beginning of my practice of gratitude.

I would not have called it gratitude back then, and it was quite some time before gratitude lists and journals became the widespread phenomena they are today. In fact, had anyone suggested I start a gratitude list in those early, turbulent years, I might have reacted with outright hostility. It felt like I was clutching at straws, desperately searching for any sign that life still held meaning. This practice was born out of sheer necessity, a lifeline thrown into the depths of despair.

Twenty somewhat years ago, I had no interest in the science behind my actions. It was a classic case of "fake it 'til you make it." It's strange how in the midst of the most crippling pain imaginable, moments of deep appreciation still sneak in. I would cling to those moments like a toddler with a lollipop: The gentleman who held the door for me so I could push my stroller through. Hearing the laughter of my eight-year-old when he would momentarily forget his sadness and be a carefree kid again. By grasping onto these moments, I was unintentionally training my brain to see the possibilities instead of dwelling on the problems.

Nothing changes perspective faster than purposefully choosing where we will focus our attention. All I knew at the time was that focusing on one current positive aspect of my life fueled my inspiration and motivation, providing me with a sense of purpose. I wasn't swimming in grief. Sometimes, I wonder what would have happened to me if I didn't do this. It scares me to think of what my life and my children's lives would look like if I allowed the painful emotions and the devastating reality to swallow me whole.

Almost a decade later, when I was working in the inpatient military wellness unit, I recognized the desperation, the painful loss of self and the hopelessness that accompanies PTSD. It was what I had felt years before. *What is there to live for? How can I go on?* I remembered what had worked for me.

Besides teaching yoga and breath work, I started handing out small notebooks. I asked each service member to list three things they were grateful for each day. If one day was particularly hard, they should list five. You could imagine the response I got from some of these combat-hardened men. They thought it was some woohoo voodoo stuff. Luckily, most of them trusted me, and the rest were respectful enough to humor me.

Every week, I would spend some time allowing them to share what they had been thankful for. Answers were simple. *I woke up this morning. I'm still breathing. I slept last night. I spoke to my wife.* Oftentimes, the answers were all the beautiful ordinary moments in our lives we take for granted—eye opening.

Occasionally, someone had a very rough week and would come up empty handed in the gratitude department. They may have even been angry or resentful I was asking them to find some good in the shit sandwich they had been served. We would work through it together finding something, anything, that would offer some hope. Many people say hope isn't a plan. When we are in the deep end of trauma and loss, we aren't looking for a plan. We are simply trying to survive long enough to see the shore.

During this period, I discovered my experience with gratitude was not an isolated incident. The same seismic shift I underwent was reflected among the men of Holliswood, a revelation that took me by surprise, particularly the rapidity of the change. The deliberate act of acknowledging the positives in our lives led to a noticeable shift in attitude and perception within merely two weeks. Signs of this change were evident: an uplifted outlook, a burgeoning sense of hope, the curve of a smile, a newfound tranquility, and the energy to act. While my observations were not grounded in formal scientific research but rather anecdotal evidence, the consistency of these experiences lent them credibility. They echoed my personal journey toward healing, reinforcing my conviction in the power of gratitude as an invaluable tool in navigating life's challenges.

I started studying gratitude because I wanted to know the why and how. This is the beauty of being both a yogi and a nurse. You strive to find the crossroads where science and spirituality meet. I learned the effects of gratitude are not coincidental at all.

I was surprised to learn about extensive research on the positive effects of gratitude on our mental, emotional, and physical health. Scientific research supporting anecdotal evidence was validating and also spurned a deep curiosity in me. I learned we aren't capable of feeling fear and gratitude simultaneously. This is when the pieces of puzzle started to come together. Like most any true healing modality, the magic of gratitude lies in the effects it has on our nervous system.

■

CHAPTER 13

Calming the Storm

When I talk about gratitude, I want to emphasize I am not talking about being grateful for our loss or traumatic experience. I am simply talking about noticing the beautiful moments still happening amid the pain. I am also not suggesting we deny our grief or bypass any emotions that may come from that grief. I am suggesting that we are amazing humans capable of holding all of these *huge* emotions simultaneously.

According to Robert A. Emmons and Michael E. McCullough, gratitude defies easy classification.[1] Gratitude has been defined as "the willingness to recognize the unearned increments of value in one's experience."[2] A grateful response to life circumstances may be an adaptive psychological strategy and an important process by which people positively interpret everyday experiences. The ability to notice, appreciate, and savor the elements of one's life has been viewed as a crucial determinant of well-being.[3] These statements all seem to support the hypothesis made by Emmons and McCullough in their 2002 study that investigated the correlation between gratitude and psychological and physical well-being. I observed this in myself and others.

Gratitude transcends mere positive thinking. It fundamentally influences our nervous system. By nature, we're wired to prioritize our problems, a trait rooted in our primal instinct to safeguard our well-being. This vigilance serves us by highlighting potential threats, allowing us to return to a state of calm once the danger has passed. However, trauma can disrupt this balance, leaving our minds in a perpetual state of alert, wary of repeating past harms. This state of hypervigilance, while once protective, can eventually undermine our well-being, affecting our sleep, digestion, and relationships. Cultivating gratitude requires a deliberate mental shift, an effort to sift through life's challenges to uncover even the smallest of joys. By doing so, we can alter our body's response, transitioning from a state dominated by fear and the fight-or-flight reaction to one of tranquility and the "rest and digest" response, fostering a sense of safety and peace.

Science has proven that gratitude lowers our heart rate. In a 2017 study by Kyeong et al., participants were asked to picture their mother and tell her in their mind how much they love and appreciate her. They found that heart rate decreased significantly compared to the nonintervention group. In this study, the nonintervention group was asked to focus on a moment or person that made them angry.

In comparing the gratitude versus "resentment" groups, researchers concluded, "Our results suggest that gratitude intervention modulates heart rhythms in a way that enhances mental health." The same study found, "When practicing gratitude, the amygdala's activity under the limbic system—responsible for processing emotions and memories—seems to be positively impacted." These results could be seen via MRI imaging.[4]

You can try this on your own and feel the impact it has on your overall well-being. Close your eyes. Envision someone you love dearly, someone who makes you smile at the mere thought of them. Do a mental scan of your body and notice how you feel. Are you relaxed? Do you feel light, maybe even expansive? Are the corners of your mouth slightly curling up?

Now switch that thought to someone who really gets your blood boiling. Notice the tightening in your muscles. Your breathing may be slightly more shallow or your heartbeat quicker. Your palms might even become sweaty and your thoughts racing. Our thoughts and emotions clearly affect our biology.

Gratitude is the ability to control where we place our attention. When we feel we have no control, it is an invaluable tool that helps bring us back to our own power. It is also a learned behavior—a skill, I dare say. I was not raised a "glass half full" girl. *Oh, noooo…* I was raised a "If we didn't have bad luck, we would have no luck" type of girl.

Gratitude did not come easily or feel natural to me. Every morning was a struggle… until it wasn't. Without realizing it, I had made gratitude a habit. This is what I mean by training our brains. I did it so often and for so long, it became the path of least resistance for my brain. When I would encounter an issue or have a difficult day, I would look for the lesson or the silver lining. It never failed me.

I did learn some tricks, though. I couldn't simply list what I was grateful for. Saying I am grateful for my health, my family, and my home is easy. To create a list from my head didn't always work the way I wanted. It felt rote. I was merely reciting the parts of my life I was expected to be happy about. I learned that for gratitude to be a power tool, I had to *feel* the gratefulness. I had to visualize what I was grateful for until I felt it in my body.

My being would become filled with a deep sense of appreciation. It would often bring me to tears thinking of someone holding a door for me, so I could maneuver my bulky double stroller through when it took all my strength to get out the door with three children for a damn container of milk. Or the time a butterfly landed on my arm and wouldn't leave after I begged for a sign Jeff was with me. The feeling of gratitude was the key to the shift. It didn't matter what I was grateful for as long as I allowed that to wash over me.

I found out later that when I shared my grateful moments with others, it made those feelings even stronger. When people joined in on my appreciation for the little but impactful things, it made the sense of gratitude spread even more. My joy became their joy. I have to tell you, this felt freaking amazing. I had spent months with my sorrow being everyone's sorrow. You tend to feel like a burden after a while. Bringing others joy or modeling a deeper appreciation for life felt authentic. It became a way to give back for all that was given to me when I needed it most.

Ah, gratitude! It is a safe space for everyone, available to all at any given moment. Yet its true power is unlocked only through deliberate choice. We must be fully present in our lives to tap into this invaluable resource. It demands not just acknowledgment but a deep, heartfelt embrace. And then, the final step in the journey of gratitude is to extend it beyond ourselves, toshare this gift with others, thereby amplifying its reach and impact in the world around us.

CHAPTER 14

Radical Acknowledgment and Acceptance

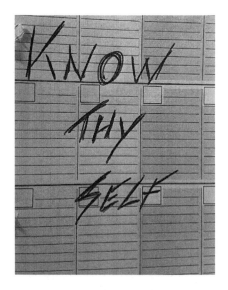

Grief and trauma have a remarkable way of peeling away the layers of our identity, leaving us exposed and vulnerable. Until September 10, 2001, I lived within the comforting roles of Jeff's wife, a nurturing mother, and a dedicated nurse, balancing work on a per diem basis at a nearby hospital. Our life was deeply rooted in the traditions of a hard-working, middle-class upbringing.

As the eldest sibling in my family, responsibility was second nature. Our home, nestled in a community of first responders and your average middle-class families, was a testament to the dreams we were gently crafting. It was more than just a neighborhood; it was where Jeff grew up and hoped to raise our children. Our aspirations were simple yet significant—making our home larger to accommodate more kids, exploring the world when our finances would permit, and reveling in the simplicity of weekend fishing trips. Surrounded by a tight-knit circle of family and friends, our lives were filled with shared moments and collective dreams. But in an instant, Jeff's absence shattered every part of our existence, catapulting me into an unrecognizable life in stark contrast to the one I kissed goodbye that fateful afternoon he left for work.

Accepting this new life did not come easily. I hadn't wanted a new life. In fact, all I wanted was to be able to turn back time. Every time I watched the replay of the plane crashing into the tower, I wanted to yell at him to get out. I devoted endless hours to scrutinizing news broadcasts, straining to read the names inscribed on the firefighters' bunker gear, hopeful for a glimpse of OLSEN. As mentioned earlier, I quickly became aware of a jarring discord between my rational thoughts and emotional responses. This clash underscores the inherent challenge of acceptance. Our brains are wired in a way that propels us toward a state of wishful thinking, a euphemistic term for denial, almost instinctively.

Creating stories that soften the blow of a tragic loss is not uncommon. The part that blows my mind, in hindsight, was how logical it all felt in the moment, at least to me. I would imagine Jeff had suffered a terrible case of amnesia and was lying in a hospital bed, unidentified. He would eventually find his way home. I had called every area hospital hoping this was the case. Months later, I would think I heard his key in the lock, returning from work as if nothing had ever happened.

Acknowledging the current state of my life and accepting he would never be coming home were critical steps for me to begin healing and moving forward. I describe this process as "radical" because it demands confronting and owning the full tide of pain, sorrow, and grief that such acknowledgment and acceptance bring, particularly the darker emotions we instinctively shy away from or, even worse, become ensnared by.

More than just accepting his passing, I had to face and embrace the entirely new existence that his absence shoved me into. This involved relinquishing the notion that life could somehow proceed as it had when Jeff was still with me, an impossibility. In practical terms, I was only one person tasked with the monumental challenges of managing a household and parenting three children single-handedly. I remember thinking for a very long time, *This is not what I signed up for with you, Jeff.*

The aftermath of trauma or loss brings collateral losses that often go unrecognized. Many other relationships in my life were deeply impacted. As I said earlier, individuals I had counted on for support faltered while unexpected figures emerged as guardian angels. It became essential for me to recognize and accept the deep changes in every facet of my life. Emotionally, mentally, spiritually, and financially, the person I was before was gone. The person I believed I was, the life I believed I had curated, no longer existed. In its place was emptiness—a blank slate.

A grasping happens when we lose someone or something. We desperately hold on to anything that creates a feeling that what we lost is not really gone—the old T-shirts, letters, photographs. We grasp on to these belongings and hold on to memories for dear life. I never cleaned out Jeff's closet or nightstand until I chose to sell the house we lived in together. As I was clearing out the nightstand, I found socks with holes and briefs that should have been thrown away while he was still alive! I laughed at myself for holding on to these things for years.

I had just not been ready to let anything that belonged to him go. All of this grasping and holding on keeps us stuck. There comes a time when we must let go. The letting go does not mean we are forgetting. It is simply another level of acknowledgment and acceptance. Holding on to old underwear did not keep Jeff's memory alive for me. He lived on in us.

I heard him in my daughter's laughter. I saw him in my son's smile and scowl because he is his twin—not just in looks but in behavior. I see him in the way my oldest carries the title of Dad now. Eventually, with some discernment and clarity, we gently loosen the grasp, realizing it will not erase what once was. This is the point where memories begin to bring more smiles and less tears.

The gift of radical acknowledgment and acceptance is that it allows us to let go of the unnecessary suffering caused by resisting or denying our reality. It allows us to embrace a more compassionate and open mindset. It is *not* approval for our circumstances, but it is knowing we cannot change what has happened. Our pain then becomes the guide to what requires our attention.

Like every other part of the healing journey, it is necessary and appropriate to take baby steps. Our hearts and minds are not capable of digesting a loss in one fell swoop. Hence, the beauty of denial. We acknowledge and accept it in small doses. A perfect example of this happened during the first Christmas season after Jeff died. The last thing I wanted to do was to put up a Christmas tree, but what felt worse was how my children would feel if we didn't celebrate. *Where did Santa go?*

So, with the help of my family, I set out to make Christmas somewhat special. I began to pull our decorations down from the second story of our garage but quickly realized the bins were too heavy for me to manage alone. Jeff had packed them thinking he would be taking them down. This felt like a knife to my chest, reminding me this was life moving forward. I was angry, sad, and defeated.

That year, I had plenty of hands to help me, but being fiercely independent, I couldn't stand the idea of having to ask for help every year. I acknowledged this was my truth in the moment. I accepted that from here on out, I would be responsible for the packing and unpacking of our decorations. I would need to be able to do this alone. After I accepted this truth, it was an easy fix.

I packed smaller, more manageable bins. This doesn't mean the next Christmas was a walk in the park—far from it. But I *was* able to get the decorations out by myself, and that was a win, a step in the rebuilding process. It was small, but it was mighty. The same happened after the first snowfall when I had to shovel myself out. I cried the entire time, remembering how Jeff would get up early to clean off our cars and shovel out our elderly neighbors. When I was done, I felt like Superwoman! I had done it. I was capable. I was alive. I was surviving.

We never know our own limits until we push past our normal routine. These baby steps I took when I would acknowledge and accept what my life had become expanded that window of tolerance. Those moments showed me I could do so much more than I had ever given myself credit for. I would break through one barrier only to be met with another over and over again. I would try to show up every single time. I didn't always win. *But* I did always learn. Traumatic grief offers us a very undiluted or concentrated experience of developing resilience. What you experience in your day-to-day life after trauma is what people learn and experience over the course of their lifetimes. The level of growth we can attain after loss is exponential. It is also very painful.

CHAPTER 15

This Is My Life

Embracing radical acknowledgment and acceptance is arguably the most challenging phase of healing. It's important to note the healing strategies encapsulated by the GRACE acronym are not designed to follow a sequential or specific order. Healing is inherently nonlinear and deeply personal. Our journey through loss and the subsequent acceptance of our reality unfolds in fleeting, nuanced moments. The evolution within us as we navigate this process is frequently gradual and unnoticeable in the moment. Only upon reflection can we truly appreciate the extent of our adaptation and growth.

The emptiness and perceived meaninglessness that trauma and loss create strip us of all the programming, learned behaviors, and beliefs that life has imprinted upon us. This stripping down creates a window through which we are given a glimpse into our own soul. This peek into yourself, your deepest desires, and your innate purpose is the gift of grief. We revisit and refine this sacred space over and over again in the grieving process.

Although it may feel like we are shoveling shit uphill, we are making progress. We are delving deep into our essence, unearthing our personal truths and reconstructing ourselves on a foundation of lived experience. We do this by examining our entire lifestyle and belief system, letting go of what no longer resonates with our evolving selves and embracing the truths that harmonize with our soul's core. These enduring beliefs fortify us, enhancing our sense of self. We are building our foundation intentionally and purposefully. It becomes unshakeable.

All of this begins with radical acknowledgment and acceptance. What exactly do these terms mean? How are they distinct from one another? Acknowledgment refers to seeing things as they are, whether we like them or not—the owning of painful truths. Acceptance involves being at peace with the reality we are in.

For me, acknowledgment was, "Jeff is not coming home." You may think this statement is obvious. How could anyone survive being buried under 120 stories? The idea that I believed he could survive for a month in that pile is an example of my brain protecting me from the crushing pain of reality. Acknowledgement comes before acceptance. Acceptance was moving his worn-out sneakers away from the front door because he would no longer be wearing them.

Radical acknowledgment and acceptance begin with self-awareness. We must first identify when we are creating unnecessary suffering for ourselves. I often found myself saying, "This isn't fucking fair," "We didn't deserve this," or, "He had so much living to do." I bet these sound familiar. These were my signs that I was going down the rabbit hole of useless suffering. While all these statements are true, they cannot be changed.

I would let myself have my "what the fuck" moments. Those are the moments of acknowledgment. It is imperative all emotions are acknowledged and allowed to come up and move through you. Yes, this may make for a shitty day. That's okay. We need to feel it to heal it.

Owning reality, radical acceptance, can really suck sometimes. These were my most crippling moments. I would find myself in bed or on the couch all day. I let that be what it was. I gave myself that space. It takes quite a lot of energy to surrender and accept that which we have never anticipated or desired in our lives. When I felt I'd had enough, I would reframe the pain that came with resisting the truth. What was I grasping onto? Where could I find even a small amount of acceptance? Could I do something different? How could I turn that painful experience into something that served me? I would get curious. I would find solutions. I would adapt.

It took me quite some time to feel as if I had made progress with my own healing journey. I felt like I was riding a rollercoaster of emotions and never getting anywhere. I believe it was because the changes I made were so small that they felt almost imperceptible. Only in hindsight was I ever able to recognize how far I had gotten.

It is important to take the time to look back and compare where we are to where we were. You will be astounded at how far you have climbed when you keep taking small baby steps in the direction of where you want to be. Even if you aren't sure what that looks like, you can be certain you will know the places and the people you have outgrown. Keep moving forward. Keep accepting your current reality and focus on the reality you would like to create.

Much like gratitude, this became a habit for me. Radical acknowledgment and acceptance allowed me to accept my present moment while also knowing I could mold that moment into whatever I would like it to be. In fact, this tool made me realize every single moment of my life mattered. I was responsible for choosing happiness. I may not have had any control over certain circumstances in my life, but I certainly had control over the way they would play out in my future.

Radical acknowledgment and acceptance break the cycle of denial. This tool taught me to be brutally honest and accountable to myself without judgment or criticism. It paved the path for creating meaning from loss. Without the brutal honesty of acknowledgment and acceptance, we would not be capable of moving forward in our lives.

CHAPTER 16
Action

In the GRACE model, action has two distinct parts. The first part is the intentional forward movement toward rebuilding your life—the building of the proverbial "new normal." The second is physical movement. I cannot stress the importance of this enough. Trauma gets stored in all the nooks and crannies of our bodies. Physical movement helps us to release them before they manifest as illness or disease.

Prior to suffering the loss of my husband, I lived a very structured and rote life. Like most adults, my day began with coffee, a shower, putting on my nursing uniform, and taking the same daily route to work. I was on autopilot. It wasn't until I was many years into my healing journey that I realized how much I had missed out on in those moments. I was moving from habit rather than conscious intention. Of course, Jeff and I had goals. We wanted to expand our home, start a college fund for the kids, and plan for our lakefront home after retirement. Goals are very different from intention.

A goal is a specific, measurable, and often time-bound objective that one strives to achieve. It is outcome-focused, providing a clear endpoint or result an individual aims to reach. Goals are concrete, such as running a marathon, earning a degree, or achieving a professional milestone. They offer a tangible target to work toward and can be broken down into smaller, actionable steps.

In our pursuit of goals, we often overlook the beauty in everyday moments, slipping into monotony and losing our sense of presence. Goals are future-oriented. The shock of grief or loss confines us to the present, as the future becomes daunting to plan and the past turns into a painful echo of what we've lost, leaving us to navigate each moment as it comes. Goals may also lead to feelings of failure or inadequacy if they are not reached as planned. There is certainly a place for goals in our grief. They provide direction and a sense of control.

Intention is more about the mindset or the underlying purpose behind actions rather than a specific outcome. Intentions are guiding principles for how you want to be, live, and show up in the world, both for yourself and in your relationships. They are less about measurable achievements and more about the quality of your journey, such as living with gratitude, kindness, or mindfulness. Intentions set a direction or a way of being that can influence multiple areas of life without being tied to a specific achievement or timeline. Goals and intention both require action.

The morning of September 11, when I realized my husband had responded to what was the worst terrorist attack on American soil, my brain instantly began to keep me safe. I dissociated. I was unable to focus. I was not thinking rationally, even though it felt as if I was. I paced in circles. I went numb to the point of being paralyzed. Voices seemed like they were in the distance—taking time to make their way into my conscious understanding.

I felt as if I was lost outside my body, even though I could feel myself in the room. Time slowed down to a painful trickle. Minutes became hours. People were asking questions I could not answer. My nervous system had completely collapsed. This would be devastating for anyone but especially for me at that time, with my lack of coping skills.

Simultaneously, there was a small voice inside of me. The survivor. The little girl who had been through so much. This voice knew I had the ability to make it through. I just didn't know the steps. What I did know was that no matter how I felt, I had to keep moving forward for the sake of my children.

My first intentional action step after 9/11 was to seek guidance and tools for coping. That's when I found Mariann, my therapist. Mariann had specific quotes she would use regularly. I affectionally referred to them as "Mariannisms." A favorite of mine was, "The universe provides."

Mariann was the embodiment of this. She was a light, not just for the grieving woman I was then but also for the inner child within me. Mariann offered me a safe place where I was heard. Goddamn, that woman listened to me for hours. Our sessions offered me the invaluable gift of feeling seen and validated. Her chair was the place I would go to express my emotions, sparing those around me from bearing the brunt of my pain at inopportune moments.

The more we talked, the more I unearthed what I liken to "Pandora's box." Initially, I sought Mariann's help to navigate the devastating loss of my thirty-one-year-old husband, but I soon realized that true healing required confronting a lifetime of buried traumas and abandonment issues. The myth of Pandora's box, where opening the box unleashed untold afflictions onto the world, resonated with me. In the depths of that box, just as in the myth, lay hope—signifying the beginning of a profound journey toward healing and renewal.

As I engaged in conversations with Mariann, we began to unveil the history of my life and all emotions I had kept hidden away. Facing these truths was more terrifying than anything I had ever encountered, demanding a level of bravery I wasn't sure I possessed. Coming face to face with your own shadow requires courage of the utmost level. Mariann provided a safe, nonjudgmental space, guiding me to adopt the same compassionate stance toward myself.

The journey was arduous, filled with moments when I was tempted to quit, to cancel sessions, or to feign forgetfulness. I mean, I am pretty sure I did a couple of those things in an attempt to dodge the discomfort of bringing light to my own darkness. She would tell me, "What are you afraid of? It's only you. You survived it all already."

Mariann was well-acquainted with the terrain of this challenging journey. She understood the limitations of words, the inevitable fear, and the necessity of tangible tools for healing. Trauma is held in the body. You will never think or talk your way out of it. Being a woman who was way ahead of her time, Mariann introduced me to the healing potential of energy work and salt baths, recommended acupuncture, and encouraged journaling as a form of self-reflection. Above all, she reinforced the powerful notion there was nothing to fear. My memories were simply fragments of experiences I had already survived, including the profound loss of my husband.

Most of us don't know where or how to begin taking positive action. Mariann meticulously constructed a pathway of incremental steps, a staircase I needed only to have the courage to ascend. The choice to move forward, to actively engage in the healing process, lay in my hands. All I needed to do was trust her and take action.

With every step I took, I discovered more about myself—my strengths, my weaknesses. I understood why I reacted and acted in certain ways. I learned about patterned behavior. This journey taught me the difference between self-care and being selfish, the grace of forgiveness, and the value of self-worth. I practiced giving myself what I needed, and I started learning to build boundaries instead of walls.

I was empowered, but we know healing isn't linear. One day I could conquer the world, and the next day I could be lying in bed with a pillow covering my head to shield me from another anniversary of 9/11. Traumatic grief goes on for a lifetime. We aren't miraculously healed. No one could do that for me, not even Mariann. She did give me the tools to ride the waves, though, and I will forever be indebted to her for that. In fact, she is one of the main reasons I decided to do this work. I want to be the lighthouse for others like she was for me.

After eight long years of therapy, my biggest takeaways were intention, getting out of my comfort zone, and having the power to do and be anything I dreamed of. What did I want my life to look like? How did I want to feel? Who did I want to be? What mark did I want to leave on this world? What was I willing to do to get there?

Once I set an intention, I would take small steps in that direction without any expectation of an outcome. I tried all sorts of new things. In fact, that was how I stumbled into a yoga class.

I only went because I had been working out like crazy and needed a good stretch. I had no idea what yoga entailed. Two decades ago, it wasn't popular the way it is now. I was in my era of trial and error. I was into getting out of my comfort zone. So, I walked into a hot yoga class clad in sweatpants. I thought I would die. I could barely do any of the poses being done so gracefully by all the half-naked women in the one-hundred-plus degree class. The only thing that kept me in that class was my ego. I was too embarrassed to walk out.

To my dismay, at the end of class, I had tears streaming down my face. I had no idea why. They felt strange—not sad, not happy. They felt like a release. And you know by now I am not a crier. Yet I found myself in a room full of strangers with uncontrollable tears falling out of my eyes. Thank God I was so damn sweaty, because no one could tell.

That isn't the craziest part. The craziest part is that I got into my car, and I was happy—for no reason. I felt like I was on a cloud. I hadn't felt this in the two years since Jeff was gone. I didn't feel that heaviness I had grown accustomed to. I was light. I wasn't sure if it was because time was marching on or if it was yoga. I went back. Same feeling, every-single-time. It pulled my mental, physical, emotional, and spiritual bodies together, and I was healing.

I knew I was healing, because everything felt balanced. I was able to be present in my body and my life in a way I hadn't been in a very long time, possibly ever. All the work was beginning to pay off. Moving my body and breath in the delicate dance of yoga was like pressing fast forward on my therapy. I had found the portal to something I never knew existed—a completely different way of life. I could control emotions and move energy within my body through movement and breathwork. It was magical. It changed the trajectory of my whole life.

Yoga, for me, was the pinnacle of the part of action that requires movement. The sequential poses coupled with breathwork and mantras creates the perfect environment for releasing deep-seated trauma. Any kind of movement is helpful.

As my yoga practice deepened, so did my boldness and desire to venture into new experiences, each step taken with profound intentionality. The significance of intention became crystal clear to me: Every decision, every action in life stems from a place of love or fear. I had spent my entire life choosing from fear: a fear of losing something or someone, a fear of failure, a fear of not being good enough, a fear of not having what I needed, a fear of being hurt or taken advantage of... The list is as long as a CVS receipt.

I was dodging and weaving through life, waiting for the other shoe to drop. I had been trapped in a cycle of reactive thinking and behavior. Intention taught me to choose from love. It extracted me from the autopilot mode and anchored me firmly in the present. It taught me to acknowledge pain while simultaneously embracing my capacity for healing. Intention revealed to me the duality of vulnerability and strength, empowering me to be the architect and narrator of my own life's story. Love is the energy that fuels our actions when we are moving through the portal that transforms our pain into power.

CHAPTER 17

Movement and Intention

Traumatic grief assaults our mind, body, and soul. We aren't only working on surviving grief. We are looking to create the portal that allows us to build a life we love living again. This is the basis of the healing model presented in GRACE.

A common misconception is that grief is purely an emotional response. But humans do not operate effectively in a compartmentalized way. What we experience in our body is embedded in our brain and reflected in our emotions. What we experience in our brain becomes embedded in our body if we don't work through our experiences. When we attempt to compartmentalize our emotions, hide away our pain, or ignore the thoughts that haunt us, we initiate the disease process.

An article posted by University of California, San Diego's Center to Advance Trauma-Informed Health Care states:

> From our extensive trauma-related research, we now recognize that unaddressed trauma is the hidden cause of most preventable illnesses and is associated with eight

of the ten leading causes of death, including heart, lung, and kidney disease, cancer, stroke, diabetes, suicide, and accidental overdose. When we fail to address the trauma that underlies these diseases, prevention and treatment is far less effective, and in some cases, not effective at all.[1]

To make matters more difficult, trauma is cumulative. Experiencing one traumatic event has a huge impact, but when we have experienced multiple traumatic events, the impact becomes increasingly more debilitating. This is noteworthy because when we speak of trauma being cumulative, we aren't only talking about major traumas such as loss of a loved one or a life-changing injury. Cumulative trauma includes the smaller events some people may not even label as trauma, such as financial loss or interpersonal relationship issues. Trauma is not a specific event; it is a person's interpretation and internalization of a specific event. This includes trauma we may not be able to remember, especially those that occurred in childhood.

Potentially traumatic experiences that occur in childhood are known as adverse childhood experiences (ACEs). ACEs were developed after an accidental finding by Dr. Vincent Felitti in his weight loss clinic in San Diego. The weight loss program had an unusually high dropout rate. What was odd was that the people who were dropping out had lost a significant amount of weight on the program already. The dropouts would then gain an obscene amount of weight back, hundreds of pounds. The common denominator was childhood trauma. Dr. Felitti presented his findings at a conference in 1990. The findings appeared significant enough for the CDC to propose a large-scale study.[2]

The clinic where Felitti had been working was the perfect sample. This was the beginning of the ACE study at Kaiser Permanente San Diego, where, each year, they could easily ask more than twenty-six thousand consecutive adults seen in the Department of Preventive Medicine if they would be interested in helping us understand how childhood events might affect adult health status. Sixty-eight percent of this population agreed to participate.[3]

The findings were groundbreaking. More than half of the participants reported two or more adverse childhood experiences. People who had experienced four or more ACEs had an increased risk for alcoholism, drug addiction, depression, and suicide. They were more likely to smoke, have self-reported poor health, high numbers of sexual partners and STDs, and increase in physical inactivity and severe obesity. The number of categories of adverse childhood exposures showed a graded relationship to the presence of adult diseases, including ischemic heart disease, cancer, chronic lung disease, skeletal fractures, and liver disease. The seven categories of adverse childhood experiences were strongly interrelated, and persons with multiple categories of childhood exposure were likely to have multiple health risk factors later in life.[4]

What does this have to do with traumatic grief? *Everything!* Remember, these studies were done on adults. The average age of participants was fifty-seven. Their trauma and accompanying grief had gone unprocessed for decades. It had quite literally changed their physical makeup. A striking finding was that adverse childhood experiences are vastly more common than recognized or acknowledged. Of equal importance was our observation they had a powerful correlation to adult health a half-century later.

The majority of us have likely experienced an adverse childhood event. More than likely, it has gone unaddressed, as was the case in my situation. When I lost Jeff, I had carried that trauma for the better part of thirty years. The crazy part was that I wasn't even aware of the effects this had on my health, my relationships, my self-esteem, and my coping skills, which were entirely based on survival. Dissociation was my drug of choice. Man, did that make me seem tough. I could endure just about everything.

This is where the dual parts of action come in. The first part is physical movement. The objective in healing is not to change what has happened to us. That is impossible. The goal is to change how we respond and hold that experience so it plays out in a healthy way in our future. This means bringing our nervous system back to baseline while reminding ourselves that we are safe in the moment and have agency over our reactions.

When we have lived in unsafe or unpredictable environments for an extended period of time, our baseline becomes a dysregulated nervous system. We do not even realize we are dysregulated. We believe this to be our normal. How do we bring awareness to this state of unrest? Through introspection. How do we shift ourselves? Well... through all of the steps outlined in GRACE. The physical body, though, requires intentional movement. It requires *action* aimed specifically at regulating our nervous system.

In Bessel van der Kolk's book, *The Body Keeps the Score*, the body is the portal to healing soul wounds.[5] Trauma gets stuck in our bodies, and no amount of talk therapy can heal that. This is because when we are traumatized, the part of the brain that allows us to verbalize is shut down. This is evidenced when we are asked to recount events and words elude us. Have you ever been so scared you couldn't speak? I have. I was within inches of a rattlesnake, and like the scene in my nightmares when I wanted to scream but nothing came out, I was unable to form even a single word. I wanted to yell but couldn't. These weird stuttering sounds were coming out instead of words. I wanted to run, but my legs felt frozen. I was holding my breath. I forced myself to inhale, or maybe I just couldn't hold it anymore. I don't remember. That breath shot me back into my body, and I was able to move away. My nervous system had placed me in a freeze state.

Moving your body is essential. Any movement that includes a right-left motion can exponentially increase communication between the two sides of the brain. The left side of our brain is for logical thinking. The right side is for creating and nonlogical thinking. It is also where our memories of touch, taste, and smell are stored. PTSD often leads to right brain dominance. We are constantly reliving the past. Our body reacts as if we are in the past. The left brain is not effectively communicating the present moment. By stimulating both areas simultaneously, we can bring them into better alignment. Walking, kayaking, and tapping are examples of this type of movement. If you are working with a professional, eye movement desensitization and reprocessing (EMDR) is a fantastic therapy.

Another type of movement that has been found to create profound shifts in PTSD is yoga. Ten weeks of consistent yoga practice can help alleviate the symptoms of PTSD. It is a nervous system regulator. The practice of movement linked with breathing helps us to become present in the moment, hyper-oxygenate our blood cells, create a sense of safety in our bodies, and increase self-awareness. This yoga practice does not have to include bending yourself into the shape of a pretzel.

I know yoga sounds intimidating to many people because one look at Instagram and you will see attractive women in positions that don't seem humanly possible. Yoga is not meant to look like that. It is meant to be a very controlled movement pattern linked with different types of breathing. Each movement targets not only muscles but joints and organs. Ultimately, yoga works on a cellular level. The feeling of lightness I experienced after my first yoga class was not coincidental. My nervous system was tended to in a way it had never been before. I simply didn't know the science behind it at the time.

Breathwork is a powerful action tool that does not require anything. We all know how to breathe. It is accessible everywhere and at any time. There is no lack of breath work techniques. All one needs to do is a quick search on the internet, and you will find a trove of videos and articles describing different techniques that create different outcomes. Box breathing is a fan favorite because it is easy and can be done inconspicuously while effectively calming our nervous system. It begins with a complete exhale to empty out followed by a deep, slow inhale to the count of four. You then hold that inhale for the count of four. Exhale in a controlled and deliberate manner for four. Hold that exhale for four and repeat—simple.

Action (or movement) does not have to be difficult or strenuous. It simply has to be intentional and mindful. Movement done outdoors is exceptionally healing because nature is soothing. It reduces heart rate, lowers blood pressure, and even decreases the production of stress hormones. Being surrounded by the energy of the earth is grounding and offers its own medicine. Just like moving our bodies and breathing, it is available at any time, any place. We need only take advantage of the gift.

Other actions we can take that help to bring our nervous system back online and restore balance in our bodies that I have used and highly recommend are acupuncture, journaling, and salt baths. I mentioned earlier how traditional Chinese medicine, a regimen of acupuncture and herbs, were instrumental in the healing of my asthma and eczema. Both disease processes were the by-products of grief and trauma.

Journaling has long been touted as a helpful tool for decreasing the symptoms of mental health issues. Writing is a meditative movement, and journaling allows us to express emotions in a way that is cathartic. Often when I suggest journaling, people tell me they aren't good at writing. This has nothing to do with crafting a story or having strong grammatical skills. It is about allowing the feelings to flow out of your body onto the paper. It creates an outlet for release. Some people use doodling in their journals as a way to accomplish this. You can start off slowly by simply writing one sentence, anything that comes to mind, and see where that leads you. It doesn't need to make any sense. It is sort of like word-vomiting. Another suggestion would be to find journal prompts online.

Epsom salt baths are another great way to regulate your nervous system. The warm water creates a feeling of safety and security. The Epsom salt releases magnesium, which is a natural muscle relaxer. Dimming the lights and listening to a guided meditation is something I do regularly.

One of the most powerful daily practices for regulation of your nervous system is meditation. Physically, it activates your parasympathetic nervous system, which lessens anxiety and stress. In my personal practice, I found that putting time aside to simply sit in silence created space for emotions to rise up and be acknowledged. It also was a time when my intentions took on a clearer picture. I was able to visualize what I wanted my life to look like. I gained an overall sense of well-being and clarity by encouraging a connection to my deepest self.

We can take many actions to regulate our nervous systems, create a feeling of safety and security in our bodies, and encourage mindfulness and self-exploration. Most importantly, they must be infused with intention.

The second part of action is forward movement with the intention to rebuild our lives. Remember when I spoke of baby steps? Here they are again. Losing our partner, our child, our job, our home, even a limb suddenly changes everything. It feels like someone picked you up out of your cozy life and dumped you in the middle of no-man's-land, shouting, "Good luck!" as they drove off into the sunset. Nothing is familiar. Most of us have no idea where to begin. I don't believe I am alone in this. Trial and error. After all my old coping skills failed, I needed to come up with some new tricks. I knew from the get-go that I had no idea how to handle this. Thank goodness for Mariann.

Taking intentional baby steps guides you precisely to where you're destined to be, especially when they're rooted in love. Actions inspired by love are invariably right. Leading with the heart, rather than the mind, ensures we stay true to our path. Our innermost being and ultimate purpose communicate through the language of love while fear and overthinking tend to shut this communication down. These small, deliberate steps evolve into significant strides as we continuously affirm our capabilities, reinforcing a belief in our own strength.

Trusting our intuition brings its own form of empowerment. The more attentively we listen, the more pronounced our intuitive voice becomes. The more we respect its guidance, the deeper our self-trust grows. For those of us healing from trauma or loss, often a wound of betrayal begins to mend as we consistently support ourselves. This consistent self-support teaches our inner child that the adult we've become is a reliable protector and ally. This journey fosters a deep-seated trust in ourselves, affirming we are indeed our own best guardians.

In my personal journey, I began by being intentional with who I surrounded myself with. I didn't have much energy on reserve, so I chose to surround myself with people who made me feel safe and supported rather than drained and further traumatized. I slowly started to create new routines that worked for me as a single parent.

I began focusing on my physical health, incorporating movement and meditation. This was daunting at first because grief makes you want to lie around. You feel so heavy. I would feel better after, and that feeling became my motivation. Start off slow. The smallest changes make a very big difference. Eventually, I sold my house and moved to New Jersey. You can sense the snowball effect. I started saying, "Hell yeah!" to everything that felt like a yes in my body and, "Fuck no!" to whatever didn't.

Ideas are nothing until we put them into action, but every single creation started with a simple thought. Small daily efforts to create what we desire, to heal our hearts, to pave a path for our loved ones and ourselves amount to a completely different life—a curated life, one in complete alignment with who we are. Often we don't recognize how far we have come. One step forward, two steps back—only in hindsight do we see the tremendous strides.

Trust the process. We aren't only healing ourselves. We are shifting the generational trauma handed down to us from our parents and that we can very easily hand down to our own children. This is part of the portal created by traumatic grief. Who would have thought pain could become such an elixir when we intentionally choose to allow it to alchemize us?

CHAPTER 18

Community

Shortly after September 11, my small two-bedroom Cape Cod style house was brimming with people. From the outside it may have appeared to be somewhat of a party: food, drinks, and lots of people. However, the atmosphere was far from festive. A solemn air pervaded as family, friends, neighbors, and firefighters filled the space. During this tumultuous time, their unwavering support became my lifeline, attending to my every need when I was incapacitated by grief and shock.

The thought of navigating the uncertainty of my husband's fate and managing household responsibilities without this outpouring of kindness was unimaginable. I know I was numb because I accepted the help without a fight. I remember saying, "Thank you," countless times, each time feeling as if those two words couldn't adequately express my gratitude.

The first few weeks I felt like I was drowning. Each act of kindness was a life preserver keeping me afloat for another day. My family rallied around me like a steadfast anchor: my sister became the caretaker of everyone's needs; my mother took the children under her wing; my aunt tirelessly managed the laundry; and my cousin who had witnessed the collapse of the towers firsthand would come to offer his silent strength after working overtime for the New York City Police Department. My FDNY family kept us all fed while friends and neighbors contributed in every conceivable way, be it through their time, homemade meals, financial assistance, or the creation of heartfelt memorials. Everyone pitched in to keep me and my children in a place that felt safe and supportive. We wouldn't have survived without this community effort.

Soon, I found myself seeking out someone who could truly understand what I was going through—another widow, close to my age, with children, who had navigated the treacherous waters of loss I was currently drowning in. I yearned for someone who could guide me, offering insights on the next best steps to take. Despite the overwhelming support from those around me, a sense of isolation had taken over. It seemed as though no one could grasp the depth of my pain or offer the wisdom that only comes from lived experience. My search initially yielded no results.

However, as time passed, I began connecting with other 9/11 widows through various memorials and events designed to support us and our children. The tragedy had left a significant number of young families without spouses, particularly within the firefighting community. At these gatherings, I found comfort and a shared understanding among women who were navigating similar emotional landscapes. Finding someone who knew what I was going through was a relief.

Though most of the time I met widows at fire department events, the most important person I met was a synchronistic, serendipitous story. Staten Island isn't very large. Most of the time, if you meet someone who is from Staten Island, you will have a mutual friend through six degrees of separation. In the summer of 2002, a friend was hosting a Fourth of July party. She had invited me and the kids. She had also said another woman who lost her husband, a NYC firefighter on 9/11, would be there, and she thought we would really get along. I went to the party, but we never met. I forget why. I had multiple people telling me how fantastic it would be if "Donna" and I met. Somehow, it never came to be.

A few months later, Jeff's best friend invited me to see a local band. I didn't go out often. It felt weird and awkward, as if I would be judged for not mourning properly, which did happen, by the way. This group of people, though, was a safe zone for me. They didn't judge. They let me blow off some steam, knowing that as soon as I walked back into my home, I was buried knee-deep in grief. A few moments of laughter were good for my soul. I went. I was standing by the stage when a beautiful, young, blonde woman stood next to me. We were both dancing, drinks in hand.

Out of nowhere, she busted out the move from *SNL*'s skit "Superstar" with Mary Katherine Gallagher. Hands in armpits, the sniff, all of it... If you have no idea what I am talking about—stop here! Find it on YouTube now because it makes the story even funnier and also gives you a glimpse into the magical personality I stumbled upon. I fell into a heap of laughter. You wouldn't expect this stunning woman to be so freaking hilarious. We start talking and dancing. Soon, she said she had to go because she had an infant and toddler at home. I noticed she was wearing a Maltese Cross necklace with a badge number on it. I asked her if her husband was on the fire department. She told me he was but was killed in the attacks. I was floored. I asked her name.

"Donna."

I immediately knew this was the woman our mutual friends had been trying to introduce me to. I told her I was Denise, and the two of us couldn't believe that after multiple attempts to meet at arranged places, we met randomly in a bar acting like fools.

We immediately connected. Donna was younger than me, but our children were similar ages. We spent countless hours on the phone keeping each other company when we couldn't sleep, sharing our fears, our accomplishments. We laughed. We cried. We experienced lots of firsts together. Donna knew me like no one. We understood one another. When we felt we were going crazy, we would call the other to be given a dose of support. I can say with my whole heart, I would not have survived without her. Her sense of humor is second to none. Her family became my family.

If you think the story of how we met is incredible, you need to hear this one. Donna was going through old pictures one day while cleaning out her attic. She called me and said something to the effect of, "Dee, you aren't going to fucking believe this!"

You could imagine that at this point in our lives, little could surprise us. She sent me a photo of her very pregnant self and her husband, Carl, at his graduation from the fire academy. At first glance, it was the same picture we all took at graduation, filled with pride while wearing our husband's Class A cover.

Upon closer inspection, I couldn't believe my eyes. Playing in the background of her photo was my son, Vincent! We had never realized our husbands had graduated from the academy together, let alone that we were standing right next to each other that day taking photos. It shook me.

It is a strange feeling to think people exist who we don't even know will play a huge role in our lives one day. We may walk past them in the street or stand in line together in a coffee shop. This permanently changed my perspective on life. I learned that every moment holds importance, and every interaction carries weight. It all matters, even if it feels insignificant. It underscored a sense of destiny in our connection, a feeling that, somehow, our paths were intertwined by design, meant to cross at precisely the right moments. Some call it the golden string of connection.

A magic happens when we are with people who can see us and acknowledge our pain. Sharing experiences with others who have gone through similar situations can bring comfort and reassurance. Because all the widows I was meeting had lost their husbands at the same time, none of us had any idea what we were doing. It was the proverbial "blind leading the blind." What we did know was how devastated each of us was in her own way, and we held one another up. We knew what no one else could know if they hadn't walked this path. When we thought we were losing our minds or acting crazy, we were reassured someone else had done the same thing. This is the healing power of community. You're never alone.

Mariann would tell me the universe provides, and provide it did. When the crowds had left my home and I was all alone with my thoughts and my children, my widow friends were a phone call away. We laughed, we cried, we shared stories, and we rebuilt our lives together. Traumatic grief is healed in the form of relationships. This is proven in the success of programs such as AA, different nonprofits that support veterans and Gold Star family members, victims of domestic violence, and the vast network of communities built to support people suffering from varying diseases. Find your tribe and love them hard!

CHAPTER 19

No One Heals Alone

We have arrived at what I feel is *the* single most important part of healing—community. No one heals alone. Countless studies support the idea that a good support network is the antidote to trauma. I am a firsthand example.

As evidenced in my story, community provides emotional support. Understanding, empathy, and a sense of belonging can work miracles in braving the storm of traumatic grief. Having people around who can listen, offer comfort, and validate emotions can be immensely helpful. This is the basis of mourning rituals like wakes, funerals, shiva, and many others. It helps the grieving accept the reality of the death while also starting the process of preserving the memory of the one they loved with others. It offers an opportunity for the community to show support and acknowledgment of the loss.

These community rituals can help normalize grief and trauma by recognizing these natural reactions to life-changing circumstances. When we see that others have successfully navigated similar journeys, we feel hope and encouragement. This normalization can also reduce stigma and foster open conversations about mental health and well-being.

Communities also provide practical assistance. This can range from helping with everyday tasks like cooking meals or running errands to offering childcare, transportation, or financial aid. These gestures can alleviate some of the burdens faced by someone dealing with grief or trauma, allowing them to spend more time and energy on healing. Resources and support on a wider community level can be found through local, state, and federal agencies as well as different nonprofit groups.

Research has shown that isolation is the leading cause of suicide. Loneliness is a natural part of grief, but the intense feelings experienced during this time can easily lead to separation and isolation. Being part of a community helps combat this isolation by connecting individuals with others. Communities include family, friends, neighbors, workplaces, places of worship, businesses, and support groups, to name a few. They can be in person or virtual, which makes finding community easier than ever. My belief is that if you can't find the community that fits you, create one. This is my "why" for doing the work I do. I never wanted another widow to walk this path alone. I know I don't have all the answers. I let my life and my ability to find happiness be the example, the hope, for others who walk this path.

When I speak of community and relationships, it is imperative I mention boundaries. Healthy boundaries show people how to treat us in a way that is comfortable and makes us feel safe. This is not the same as building walls and blocking people out. When we are ravished by traumatic grief, it is vital that we create boundaries. If you were not raised with boundaries, this will feel very uncomfortable for you. It will probably upset those who are accustomed to benefitting from your lack of limits.

My therapist told me I must protect my heart as if it was made of glass. It was that fragile. I was not comfortable with setting boundaries, but I knew it was necessary. I made an active effort to surround myself and my children with those who supported and cared for us. I did my best to avoid situations that would upset this delicate balance.

The pushback from others was real and often hard to navigate. I was blessed with a strong personality, but to this day I am learning how to set healthy boundaries in a loving way. It is one thing to name them and another to enforce them. Boundaries allow me to be true to myself and to have more authentic relationships.

The most important aspect of community is the strength and resilience I gained from knowing I was not alone. Knowing I had a network of people who had my back and were willing to help instilled a sense of security, which allowed me to move forward with determination. Someone was always there to catch me when I fell.

As my healing journey continued, I became a part of multiple communities in an effort to bring the hope, inspiration, and support so generously offered to me to others. When I realized yoga had exponentially sped up the healing happening with my therapist, I wanted to share it. This is how it changed the trajectory of my life.

In a very serendipitous turn of events, when I completed teacher training, I was offered a position working with service members in the inpatient military wellness unit, designed to assist those with severe and debilitating PTSD with a combination of traditional and complementary healing methodologies. Strong and Soulful was born.

I was following my gut, using my formal education, and trusting in my own personal experience when I developed Strong and Soulful yoga. After a few weeks, the results were indisputable. We expanded the program to include family members. I developed relationships within the military community and also the nonprofit sector.

This opened up one opportunity after another to inspire others while also keeping my husband's name alive.

At every event, I was asked if I had written a book. I had started many times but never felt as if my story was complete enough to share. That all changed in 2021. In honor of the twentieth anniversary of 9/11, I rucked approximately 250 miles from Logan International Airport to the WTC with my friend Danny, a retired green beret, and a seventeen-year-old named Ezra who wanted to have a deeper understanding of the events of that day.

It was the most physically and mentally challenging event I had ever done. As I approached the end of the life-changing hike, I was met by my now grown children, my grandson, friends I had met over the course of this twenty-year journey, and my fire department family.

When I rounded the corner and saw One World Trade Center, it hit me. Everything had changed—yet stayed the same. The city is different. I am different. Yet I am more myself than I have ever been. We made it. Not just me, Danny, and Ezra, but my family. We made it twenty years. No matter what life threw at us, we hung on—to each other, to the memories, to hope. It was a full circle moment. It was time to get it all on paper and, once again, lean into community for support. Writing is another part of my healing journey. It feels like the final step because it has been extremely cathartic, as you can imagine. But if I have learned anything, it is that this journey has no end. There is no final step. We keep evolving and sharing. Our community is who we walk with.

CHAPTER 20

Emergent Narrative

Emergent narrative suggests that everyone's path through grief is a personal, evolving story shaped by their own experiences, decisions, and responses. This narrative is formed by how we handle our emotions, the impact of our memories, and our interaction with the world around us. Its real power lies in its adaptability. As we integrate our loss into our daily lives, our story becomes more flexible and capable of change. Over time, just as a river alters the terrain it passes through, our narrative gradually reshapes, adjusting to the changing phases of our lives.

Emergent narrative brings us full circle in the healing journey. This is where we write our own story. This is where we create a legacy. In emergent narrative, we have the opportunity to memorialize those we have loved and anything we have lost. We have the opportunity to craft our own happy ending in the novel that is our lives. How will this experience play out in our future? We get to decide that. How do we prevent this traumatic event from overshadowing the beauty that still exists in our lives? We do this by sharing our stories, by being brave enough to use our voices, by creating change to prevent this from happening again, by memorializing those who were lost in a way that feels honorable and healing and celebrates their lives.

One of the most haunting images in the aftermath of the towers' collapse was the sight of deserted triage centers and emergency rooms broadcasted on the news. As a nurse with emergency room experience, I braced for scenes of pandemonium. Considering the World Trade Center housed approximately 17,400 individuals at the time of the attack, the eerie silence at nearby hospitals was overwhelming. The question loomed ominously: Where had everyone gone?

Shortly thereafter, a list was curated that recorded the roughly six thousand people whose whereabouts remained a mystery. "Unaccounted for" was the catch phrase propagated by the media, and it is forever seared into my memory. In response, families and friends of those missing took to the streets, plastering flyers adorned with the faces of their loved ones and contact information. These flyers marked the genesis of public memorials. In the immediate wake of such catastrophes, it's not unusual to witness the spontaneous emergence of tributes—photographs, candles, handwritten notes, bouquets—blanketing the site of the sorrow.

These initial memorials served as a gathering point for the community, a place where collective grief was acknowledged and support was shared, forging a bond of unity in the face of unimaginable loss.

Because my loss was a public loss experienced by our entire nation, I bore witness to spontaneous memorials made all over the country. The American flag, hoisted above the rubble, became a symbol of our undaunted spirit, a declaration that we, as a nation, would stand resilient. In every community, firehouses became focal points of tribute, adorned with impromptu memorials by the neighborhoods they protect. I, unknowingly, began creating my own memorial as well.

My journal is the earliest memorial to Jeff that I can remember. I would write down memories and dreams we shared together, mostly out of fear of forgetting them. I kept his picture at the head of our table where he sat to share meals with the family. My home organically transformed into a communal memorial, a place where friends and family congregated to honor the lives touched by tragedy and to navigate the tumult of emotions that followed. We held candlelight vigils on our front lawn and spent countless hours sharing stories about Jeff, gathering details about the site, and cursing Al-Qaeda. For the most part, this continued until I decided it was time to have an actual memorial service. I want to share the story of how I came to this decision because it was a pivotal part of my emergent narrative—a desire to integrate my loss into life.

My birthday falls on Sept 25. In 2001, I turned thirty-three. The previous two weeks had been shadowed by the harrowing hope my husband might still be found amid the ruins of the Twin Towers. In the days following the tragedy, I had been offered a chance to visit the site, an offer I initially declined. Yet as my birthday neared, a deep yearning to feel closer to Jeff grew within me. Firefighter Jimmy Molinell, who was Jeff's mutual partner at Engine 246/Ladder 169, had since become my liaison. He graciously agreed to accompany me to Lower Manhattan.

As I stepped out of the car, every single one of my senses was assaulted. There was a smell of smoldering fuel and pulverized concrete. The scent of destruction and death hung in the air like a blanket. It is a smell that only those who had been at the site have experienced, and it is a smell no one will forget.

Everything around me was shrouded in a pall of fine, grayish-white dust. Downtown New York City had become unrecognizable. This surreal environment, starkly contrasting with the vibrant city I knew, served as the backdrop to the profound sense of loss and longing that marked my birthday that year.

I had worked downtown for a number of years, and I couldn't make heads or tails of where I was standing. Buildings were spray painted with orange Xs and cryptic numbers. An incessant clanging was coming from the pile. As we approached the site, climbing over debris and equipment, I could not take in what was before me. I had spent untold hours staring at this scene on television: first, the bucket brigade's tireless efforts, men digging through the rubble with their bare hands for their brothers under the relentless glow of spotlights refusing to yield to night; eventually, heavy machinery was brought in. Nothing I saw on TV adequately depicted the reality smoldering in front of me.

The "pile" loomed ominously, a grotesque monument of destruction towering at least six stories high and surpassing the height of some city buildings. It was a funeral pyre of still-burning embers, a chaotic fusion of twisted steel, shattered glass, and colossal concrete chunks sprawling over an entire city block.

The sheer magnitude and complexity of the debris field left me with a haunting thought, *How the hell would they ever find anyone in that?* A needle in a haystack was all I kept thinking. This striking difference between what I had envisioned and the heartrending reality I now faced emphasized the enormity of the tragedy and the daunting task of search and recovery that lay ahead. It seemed an impossible mission.

I thought I would be frightened. I thought I would feel Jeff there and have my heart ripped out all over again imagining him buried underneath this wreckage. Instead, I was enveloped in a strange calm. He wasn't there. His body may be there, but his soul was free. This was one of those moments when my heart seemed to understand truths that my mind struggled to grasp. Intuition. *Withinity.* Whatever you want to call it, I recognized the need for closure, not just for me but for our children; for everyone touched by this tragedy. I felt as if they would never be able to find anyone in that mess. I also didn't want to let go of hope. I didn't want to give up on him. I didn't yet trust my own intuition.

Compelled by desperation, I went home and consulted the world wide web. I scoured the internet, trying to find stories of survival against all odds, clinging to any precedent that might mirror in some way our unprecedented situation. The closest scenario I could find was being buried after a natural disaster such as an earthquake. Someone had lived three weeks.

Knowing Jeff was an avid outdoorsman along with his fire department training, I thought if anyone could survive, it would be him. With this thread of hope, I resolved to wait four weeks before holding a memorial, setting the date for October 12. This decision was a precarious balance between honoring my intuition and clinging to the hope that Jeff's indomitable spirit might defy the odds.

The tribute of a firefighter's funeral is one of the most honorable ways we memorialize those who have made the ultimate sacrifice. The memory of the sea of blue uniforms and the helicopter formation flying overhead at Jeff's service is indelibly etched in my mind. Approaching St. Patrick's Church on Staten Island, the cloudless blue sky mirrored the clarity of that fateful Tuesday while a colossal American flag waved from the extended ladder of a local fire engine, a sight both awe-inspiring and solemn.

The throng of attendees was staggering. A sea of blue uniforms lined the streets surrounding the church. I vividly recall the innocence in my three-year-old daughter's voice as she said, "Mommy, there is so much blue." I felt eerily detached from my own body, to the point where I was afraid I wouldn't be able to walk the distance from the car to the church.

My eldest son, Vincent, clung to me in tears while other family members carried my daughter and youngest son. Despite the haze of overwhelming emotion, I somehow found my way inside the church, though my memory of the service remains fragmented. I am told that heartfelt eulogies filled the air, and I was presented with a meticulously folded flag while a helmet was placed into my son's trembling hands. Yet these moments have slipped from my grasp, leaving behind only the echo of their solemnity. I don't remember any of the service.

The funeral did not bring me the type of closure I thought it would because we didn't have Jeff's body. Instead, we had a coffin filled with everything that made him the man he was. It held his Class A uniform, his green backpack found hanging in his locker at the firehouse, fishing poles, pictures of the kids, heartfelt drawings and notes from family members, and his preferred pack of Parliament cigarettes. We even slipped a can of Budweiser in there.

While the ceremony did not seal the void left by his absence, it definitely brought a deeper level of acceptance. He would not be coming home. His sneakers were by the front door. All of his clothes were right where he had left them. His ambitious boat project towered in my driveway—so much of him but nothing at the same time.

A few weeks later, exactly forty days after the attack, the unimaginable happened: Jeff's body was recovered. I was given official notification and once again was asked to plan a memorial. This time, I was devastated. I asked to see him and was denied because of the advanced state of decomposition.

I begged. I didn't care what he looked like. I was a nurse, goddamn it. I could tolerate seeing anything. I just wanted to see his face one more time. The answer remained no. We cremated his remains and had a small graveside ceremony to bury his ashes along with the coffin we had buried only a couple of weeks earlier.

I later learned that without having the physical proof viewing a body brings, there is a profound ambiguity to grief. This ambiguity clouds the path of acceptance and closure. This sentiment is shared by families of POWs, parents of missing children, and also Gold Star spouses whose partners left for work and never returned.

With the passage of time, I came to appreciate being denied the chance to view Jeff's remains. It's as though some greater wisdom understood my needs far better than I could. Now, when I reflect on Jeff, he appears vividly alive in my mind, frozen in time, as young as he was the last time I saw him while I grow older with every passing year. Had I been confronted with the harsh reality of his remains, that image would have become my final memory of him. For that, I am beyond grateful.

As months passed, I changed. There were plaque dedications and street renamings. We took part in all of them. Months melded into years. I noticed other widows organizing events like golf outings to honor their late spouses, which left me feeling a pang of guilt for not having done something similar for Jeff. However, nothing I came across seemed to capture who he truly was.

The discourse around the redevelopment of Ground Zero began. It aimed to pay homage to a diverse group of individuals, many of whom were never recovered, making the site their final resting place. March 2006, construction began on a permanent memorial, now known as the National September 11 Memorial and Museum located at the site of the World Trade Center. It was completed and dedicated on Sept 11, 2011. Permanent memorials were also established at the other attack sites, including the Pentagon and Shanksville, serving as moving tributes to the lives lost and the resilience displayed in the face of tragedy.

While the nation crafted their story for history, I was continuing to craft my own emergent narrative. I chose to let my life be a tribute to his. I knew my purpose moving forward was to help others navigate the pain and loss that accompanies traumatic grief. Jeff's story was the foundation of that. To my surprise, an entire community wanted to support me.

When I started working with the military, I shared his story and the tools I had discovered to offer hope to those suffering the way I had. I was encouraged by so many, but one person in particular believed in my work. What I was offering at the time was not mainstream, especially in that community. Yoga and breathwork were often dismissed as fringe and lacking scientific validation.

Tina Atherall truly heard me. She grasped the profound significance of nurturing healing across mind, body, and soul. She was the cofounder of a national nonprofit organization at the time that supported our post-9/11 military. She offered me opportunity after opportunity to share my ideas and Jeff's story. My initial intention was merely to offer assistance, yet Tina perceived the broader impact and potential of my efforts. She not only encouraged me to stretch beyond my comfort zones but also extended invitations for me to present in settings that, to me, felt beyond my realm of expertise, thus broadening the impact and influence of our shared mission in healing.

I found myself addressing audiences alongside trauma experts and researchers with doctorate degrees, despite my lack of formal education in the field. My expertise was not derived from textbooks or classrooms. It was honed through personal trials. I was forged through fire. My background as a registered nurse as well as a yoga instructor provided me with extensive knowledge of human anatomy and physiology. Additionally, my nursing career had imparted a rich understanding of death, dying, and trauma in all its forms. Tina played an invaluable role in helping me recognize the value of intertwining this professional knowledge with my personal journey, highlighting the unique perspective I brought to discussions on grief, trauma, and healing.

These speaking engagements connected me to other professionals. I met a trauma expert, Bonnie Owens, who changed the way I thought about movement. Together, we created events that served to address those with PTSD in a holistic way. We saw the deep healing that would happen when we created a safe space for community and strategic movement. The shift in perspective was enormous. The sharing of stories with endings yet unwritten became stories of hope rather than devastation. These experiences molded me. They contributed to my own healing and fine-tuned my own narrative. What I learned is that wisdom always trumps knowledge, but the two together are the special sauce.

As I evolved, so did my narrative. I learned the power of storytelling, and 1 used my God-given talent of *loving to talk*. My beloved grandmother always told me I had "the gift of gab" when I was a child. It seemed as though every experience in my life had been a stepping-stone to this very moment.

My voice has found its way into podcasts and documentaries, and I've stood as the keynote speaker for a myriad of organizations. I have spoken at schools. I have shared Jeff's story with some very special people. For me, there is no greater honor than to speak his name, to celebrate his life, and to build a legacy that commemorates his sacrifice. The tribute of sharing our story in a way that offers a glimmer of hope for others not only keeps his memory alive but also enriches my journey with profound purpose and meaning.

CHAPTER 21

You Are the Meaning Maker

Traditional memorialization serves as a means to honor and preserve the memories of individuals or significant events. This practice manifests in various forms, encompassing death rituals, the creation of physical memorials and shrines, the organization of fundraisers, the establishment of digital tributes, and other acts of remembrance. Key death rituals—including funerals, sitting shiva, and cremation ceremonies—are deeply rooted in cultural and religious traditions. These ceremonies play a crucial role in uniting communities, offering a collective space to mourn, extend support, and celebrate the lives and legacies of those who have passed. Through these diverse practices of memorialization, we not only commemorate the departed but also integrate their spirit into the communal and cultural mosaic of our societies.

Why are memorials important? Trauma occurs when we feel as if we have lost our power. We are no longer in control of what happens to us. How do we change that mindset? How do we reclaim our power? In the case of family members and friends of 9/11, taking back power in the immediate aftermath of the collapse meant playing a role in locating their loved one. If you weren't permitted on "the pile," one of the ways to find your missing person was by posting their picture. The vast majority of people posted were part of the 2,753 people confirmed dead.

Another reason memorials are important is because grief creates a fear within us that what was lost will be forgotten. In the months that followed my husband's death, I would replay every inch of his face and body. I would recall the shape of his nose, his hands, the way his hair felt, the way he smelled, and the sound of his voice. I was petrified that someday I would wake up and not be able to remember the little things I loved so much. I was also afraid his way of living would be overshadowed by how he died. How could I memorialize him? How could I ensure his story lived on? This is where the emergent narrative was born.

The emergent narrative framework recognizes there isn't a one-size-fits-all path through grief. Instead, each person's journey is dynamic and personal. As we navigate through grief, we may unexpectedly uncover new strengths, forge new relationships, or adopt fresh perspectives on life previously unimagined, mirroring the concept of evolving outcomes where the journey of grief, much like life itself, can lead to unforeseen discoveries and growth.

I purposefully use the word "emergent" because the way we integrate pain and share our experiences with others changes over time. The posters seen all over downtown Manhattan were spontaneous memorials. Spontaneous memorialization is a rapid public response to publicized, unexpected, and violent deaths, typically involving the accumulation of individual mementos to create a shrine at the death site.

Most spontaneous memorials start within hours of death notification; someone leaves a candle or bouquet of flowers, which is followed quickly by contributions from others. Well-documented spontaneous memorials have appeared near mass death sites like the park overlooking Columbine High School in Littleton, Colorado (the site of fifteen fatal shootings in 1999), or the fence surrounding the Alfred P. Murrah Federal Building in Oklahoma City.[1]

If you have ever driven down any length of highway, you are sure to have seen spontaneous memorials on the side of the rode where someone may have died in a car crash. Prominent sociologist C. Allen Haney and his colleagues have noted several ways spontaneous memorials differ from traditional or permanent memorials. The first is quite obvious—there are no rules. Anyone can participate in any way they choose. Candles, flowers, pictures… any artifact an individual deems appropriate is acceptable. Second, there are no time constraints. These memorials pop up almost immediately and, in some cases, last for a very long time.[2]

You can see some of the "Lost" photos if you tour the 9/11 Memorial Museum located at the site. Another very different aspect of spontaneous memorials is the lack of expectation around ritual and ritual behavior. People freely express any emotion they are feeling. Anger and guilt are often voiced openly. When we attend a traditional death ritual, the only emotion people feel appropriate expressing is sadness.

We can create our own narrative in many ways. We can write about our loved ones. We can plant trees in their honor. We can construct memorials, hold events, create CrossFit WODs… But let it arise organically. Move in the direction that speaks to your heart. Do what feels right and honorable. Be brave enough to use your voice. Remember the most important part is that we share their stories. Use their life and yours for good.

If change needs to be created to prevent something similar from happening, do it in their honor. Many female veterans are sharing their stories of sexual abuse to create change in military policy so that other women do not have to endure what they did. This is a way to take back our own power and honor ourselves, reestablish trust in ourself, and memorialize those lost. We take our power back by choosing how the pain of this event will play out in our future. Will we allow it to destroy us, or will we turn that pain into power?

I sought out a mentor to help me dive deeper into myself and my own healing so I could create offerings for individuals who were desiring the same. I found the perfect mentor in Tiffany Carole. I was able to connect my experience to other experiences in my life. This mentorship allowed me to see how my actions create a ripple effect in the universe.

We are all purposeful creations. Everything we do either contributes to or detracts from the energy around us. We are a small, but necessary, part of a vast collective. We matter. Our experiences matter—not only to us but to others. My purpose in sharing Jeff's story and my own healing became a divine calling. I gathered more tools that were invaluable in healing my own wounds as well as those of others.

Tiffany taught me about generational trauma, how what we don't address is passed down to our children. Patterns left untended become familial patterns. I wanted more for myself and my family. This led to the creation of an online platform and mentoring. This all evolved into the book you are holding right now.

An emergent narrative is a necessity. As of this writing, we have experienced 499 mass shootings in the United States, according to the Gun Violence Archive. These resulted in thirty mass murders.[3] The numbers alone are staggering. What the statistics don't show is the number of people suffering traumatic grief as a result.

The level of trauma that occurs at any mass violence event reaches far into the community and sets the stage for generational trauma when not addressed properly. As a community, one of the first healing steps taken is the creation of memorials. They play a crucial role in the aftermath of mass violence events by providing a space for remembrance, healing, and collective grieving.

Psychologist Robert Neimeyer explains that memorials "provide a public context for the expression of grief, validating the reality of loss and inviting communal support."[4] You can see from this statement how instrumental creating memorials can be in the process of GRACE.

When we are carting memorials for any event, it is important to let those directly affected determine how their story will be portrayed. They need to feel their loved one's lives are accurately and safely preserved. When the 9/11 memorial was in the creative stages, there was so much division over how it would be done because, although it was a community event, the individual pain varied widely. Creating something that satisfied everyone was quite a feat.

When trauma strikes on an intimate level, such as in the case of a sexual assault, the process shifts from memorializing to actively seeking integration, transforming suffering into strength and reclaiming autonomy in the face of feelings like shame, helplessness, and vulnerability. This emergent narrative path can take diverse forms.

For Pam, the turning point toward her healing journey began with a service dog named Nimitz. Her decision to persistently pursue her own recovery marked the start of reclaiming her inner strength. Nimitz became the crucial element she needed, bridging the gap to recovery.

The service dog community enveloped her in the empathy and camaraderie she had longed for after years of isolation. This pivotal connection altered Pam's life's course, inspiring her to voice her experiences and extend support to others on their paths to healing. She was no longer being dragged through life; she was determining her path.

The power of emergent narrative cannot be underestimated. Resilience is born from learning that no matter what comes our way—whether we choose it or not—we have the power to determine what it means in our lives. It creates a legacy for both survivors and those lost. It evolves as we evolve.

CHAPTER 22

Signs

When we are heading in a new direction toward a place we have
never been before, we look for signs, those subtle indicators that
reassure us we're moving along the right path. Signs have been
my constant reassurance I am doing the next right thing. Plus,
they are a reminder Jeff is always near. Now, I know many of
you are probably rolling your eyes and wondering what this
hocus pocus bullshit is. I invite you to get out of your comfort
zone a bit, keep an open mind, and continue reading.

The impetus for this chapter came unexpectedly from a conversation with Jimmy Lowe, a firefighter and dear friend of Jeff's who has been a constant in my life for the past twenty years. Jimmy recently shared how deeply one of my stories about the signs I have received from Jeff resonated with him, reaffirming the powerful impact these seemingly ethereal moments can have.

Earlier in this book, I shared the story of how I found out about the planes flying into the towers. What I didn't share was what unfolded after that initial phone call. I found myself riveted to the television, wondering how the firefighters would ever get up as high as the fire and execute the rescue of those above the fire floors. The thought of the towers collapsing hadn't even crossed my mind.

I was concerned for my husband but also looking forward to him coming home to share the story of the most monumental fire of his career. My anticipation turned to shock when, at 9:59 a.m., fifty-six minutes after Flight 175's impact, the South Tower disintegrated into rubble. I couldn't believe what I was seeing.

I knew Jeff was certainly in one of the towers because his company was first due to respond to the World Trade Center. While clinging to hope that he was safe in the other tower, the reality that Jeff might be among the injured loomed large. My mind began to go into tactical mode.

I immediately recalled a conversation we shared about FDNY protocol for injured members. They would send someone to pick me up and bring me to the hospital to be by his side. I realized I better be prepared for that. I hopped in the shower with my TV blaring in the background so I could hear what was happening. As I was showering, I heard the newscaster yelling that the North Tower was coming down.

At that exact moment, a locket that Jeff had given me fell from my neck. It didn't simply slide off. I had the sensation someone had grasped on to it as they were falling, and it had snapped. A part of me knew in that instant he had fallen in that building. I refused to believe it. I picked up the necklace, assuming it would be broken. It was not. The chain was intact. The clasp was intact. I was flabbergasted. I put it back on. Forty days later, Jeff was indeed recovered from the North Tower.

There is also more to the story of my first visit to Ground Zero. I've shared how that visit gave me a gut feeling Jeff was no longer with us, nudging me toward organizing a memorial. The very next day, as I sat on my porch with the sunrise painting the sky, I found myself deep in thought, almost chatting with Jeff. I confessed to him that it felt like he had left this world, yet I yearned for some kind of assurance he was at peace.

I asked for a sign. I didn't want it to be any ordinary sign. I wanted something undeniable. I decided the sign needed to be a red-tailed hawk. I knew they weren't common on Staten Island at the time, but I would be able to easily spot one because Jeff loved them, and we would count them with the kids on road trips to Pennsylvania. I asked him out loud to send me a red-tailed hawk.

Not long after, I faced one of the most heart-wrenching days imaginable. I had been asked to swab the mouths of my children for DNA identification and list every identifying factor on Jeff's body. It shattered me. Asking my babies to open their mouths because they carried his cells in their blood and reviewing in my mind every inch of the body I hadn't seen or touched in weeks was too much. It conjured up the fear I felt when I thought of our lives without him.

I arrived back home after finishing this soul-shattering task. My house, at this point, was always filled with firemen, friends, and family inside and out. As I walked up my driveway, I noticed everyone was gazing intently up at the sky. I asked one of the firemen what they were all looking at. He pointed to a bird flying above, and he said it had been circling my house for a while. My gaze followed his outstretched arm.

There in the sky, circling gracefully with widespread wings, was the red-tailed hawk. A wave of relief washed over my entire being. I wasn't alone. He was only a thought away. On the day of his funeral, the hawk circled the church for the entire ceremony. To this day, the red-tailed hawk appears at the mere thought of Jeff. It feels like a sweet hello and a reminder that death is nothing more than moving from one state of being to another.

Finally, and a little more upbeat, we fast forward a few years. I had the opportunity to speak to a world-renowned medium. She was insisting Jeff wanted me to see a box. Jeff used to tease me he wouldn't share certain stories of his wild younger years until I was too old to leave him.

The medium mentioned this. That alone blew my mind. The problem was I had never seen any box that fit the description she was giving.

She said it was an old footlocker, and it contained everything from his life he hadn't had the opportunity to share with me. She said she was clearly seeing a multicolored blanket-like wrap with a strange erratic design on it. I kept saying none of it sounded familiar. She told me to keep it in mind and moved on with the reading. The medium said many things that day that were validating and sent me home with messages for each of my children. I left with a sense of having spent the day with him. I was on a high.

The following day, when Vincent was at school and the two babies were napping, I went out to the garage. It was a detached garage with a second-level storage space that was accessed via a ladder. I never went up there. The garage was Jeff's man cave. I would tease him that when he went out there his long hair grew back. It was the only likely place for the footlocker I had never seen before. I climbed the rickety, old wooden ladder and allowed my eyes to adjust to the dark. I looked around and could see nothing that resembled what the medium had described. I attempted to move some boxes around. Still nothing.

As I stretched and extended my arm as far as I could, I shouted at Jeff, "If you want me to find this fucking thing, you better help me!" Not a minute later, my finger ran across a piece of jagged metal. I climbed to the tippy top of the ladder, which was definitely not safe, but I needed to know. I grabbed the corner and pulled the object as much as I could.

It was heavy and slowly slid into view—the footlocker. I had to go inside and call my sister to come help me get it down.

When I finally opened it, lying across its contents was a Mexican blanket, just as the medium had described. I was breathless. Inside contained memorabilia from Jeff's entire life. There were GI Joes, old love notes, concert T-shirts meticulously folded and placed in plastic bags, albums, and the most treasured gift—old journals. Reading about his escapades, seeing his handwriting and doodles, all the song lyrics—it was one of the most valuable gifts he had ever given me.

I share these stories because if you are one of the many individuals who have asked for signs, looked for signs, or been given signs for any reason—you aren't alone, and you aren't cuckoo. The feeling of being able to communicate with those we love who have left this earth is not only comforting, it offers a sense of validation there is more to this life than we know. To this day, I receive signs from Jeff. He comes to me in my dreams. If you ever see me driving, and I am talking to an empty passenger seat, no you didn't! In all honesty, I do feel him while I'm driving. I cherish these moments. If you need a sign, I hope you ask for it, receive it at just the perfect time, and trust in what you are given.

CHAPTER 23

Only a Thought Away

In the journey of grief, the heart seeks comfort in the smallest of gestures, a search for meaning amid the echoes of loss. The experience of receiving signs from those who have passed on offers a sense of peace and a unique form of healing. These signs, often subtle and deeply personal, carry with them the potential to bridge the gap between the physical and the spiritual, providing a sense of continuity and presence that transcends the finality of death.

Signs are also known as after-death communications (ADCs). After-death communication is a spontaneous experience in which a living person has a feeling or sense of direct contact with a deceased person.[1] Signs from deceased loved ones manifest in many forms, each as unique as the individual and the bond shared. From the sudden appearance of a favorite bird or the unexpected discovery of an old memento to hearing a favorite song at the most opportune time, these moments hold a special significance. They speak a language beyond words, a communication of the soul that reassures us love endures beyond the physical confines of existence.

The therapeutic essence of these signs lies in their ability to soften the sharp edges of grief. They offer a momentary reprieve from the ache of absence, a whisper of connection in the silence of loss. These signs serve as tangible evidence our loved ones are still with us in some form, watching over and offering guidance. This reassurance can significantly ease the burden of grief, providing a comforting reminder we are not entirely severed from those we have lost.

Engaging with these signs can also serve to nurture the continuing bond with our loved one, a concept increasingly recognized for its importance in healthy grieving. Rather than moving on from the loss, we can choose to move forward with our loved ones still a part of our lives, albeit in a different form. Acknowledging and cherishing these signs can facilitate this ongoing relationship, offering a pathway through which we can maintain a connection and integrate the loss into our life narrative.

While skepticism exists, with some attributing these experiences to mere coincidences or the by-product of intense grief, the therapeutic value for those who receive them is undeniable. The key lies not in the objective proof but in the personal meaning and comfort these signs provide. In the realm of grief, where emotions reign supreme, the acceptance and validation of these experiences are pivotal in harnessing their healing potential.

What is surprising to me is the number of people who have reported having experienced signs and communications from those who have passed. ADC is quite common. In a systematic review of all research on ADC encompassing thirty-four studies between 1894 and 2006 involving over fifty thousand participants from twenty-four countries, Jenny Streit-Horn found at least one-third of people have reportedly experienced ADC at some point in their lives. Remarkably, she found rates of reported ADC to be predominantly consistent across age groups, ethnicities, genders, education levels, incomes, and religious or nonreligious affiliations. In addition to the commonality of ADC, researchers have found the grieving people who experienced it seemed as mentally healthy as the general population, and they almost always reported it brought relief from their painful symptoms of grief.[2]

For those navigating the tumultuous waters of grief, acknowledging and embracing the possibility of receiving signs can be a crucial step in their healing journey. It invites a mindset open to the extraordinary, a heart ready to receive messages of love and reassurance from beyond. In the solitude of loss, these signs emerge as silent companions, guiding the bereaved toward a place of peace and acceptance.

The therapeutic power of signs from deceased loved ones serves as a touching reminder of the enduring nature of love and the unbreakable bonds that connect us across the divide. As we open our hearts to these messages, we allow ourselves to find comfort in the knowledge that, in the dance of life and death, love remains the eternal constant.

Conclusion

On September 10, 2001, our lives were ordinary. Over the course of the past twenty-plus years, I have learned more lessons than I can count. My heart has been broken time and time again as fresh waves of grief washed over me.

One day while practicing yoga at a conference in New York City, I found myself overcome by emotion. I lay on my mat in our final pose known as savasana in a room full of strangers with tears rolling down my face. The teacher happened to be walking by, and I guess she saw or felt my emotion. I heard her voice in my ear, "You aren't broken. You're being broken open." I felt that in my soul. I share that quote with everyone.

The difference between being broken and being broken open is metamorphic. Being broken infers something is wrong with us. We are irreparably damaged. Being broken open encompasses the feeling of growth. It acknowledges the pain while also emphasizing the space created for potential. What I didn't realize at the time was that I was growing into more of myself. I was finding my highest purpose and potential. My grief gave me the opportunity to sift through every aspect of my life.

The quote, "Know thyself," inscribed at the entrance of the Temple of Apollo in Delphi, Greece, was a recurrent theme after Jeff was killed. I had found it written in one of his many notebooks, and it was traced over so many times that the ink almost tore through the paper. "Know thyself" was the journey I was thrust into. Through Jeff's death, I touched on the fragility of my own mortality. I became keenly aware I had no time for anything that was not in alignment with my values and deepest desires. This one life is certainly not a dress rehearsal.

One of the most valuable lessons I learned is that everything in this life is temporary. "This, too, shall pass" was another favorite quote of Jeff's. I remind myself of this in both good and bad times. Giving your joy and your pain equal attention is important. Similarly, it is important not to get engulfed by either of them forever.

Trauma changes us on a physical, emotional, and spiritual level. The type of change is our choice. If you come away with one thing from this book, please let it be that you have the power to *choose*! You are the meaning maker. You are the cocreator of your life.

Grief is *normal*! Hell, what does "normal" even mean? In this instance, I mean it is a universal response to losing something that mattered to us. Healing, on the other hand, is *not* universal. It is not linear. Healing cares not about time. It looks different for each of us. Please do not judge yourself or compare yourself to other people. More importantly, do not concern yourself with the judgments of other people. They have not walked in your shoes. Answer the call of your own soul.

A miracle is a simple shift in perception. Growing up Catholic, I read about incredible miracles in the Bible. I always thought a miracle was something so *huge* and obvious that you couldn't miss it. While I believe that happens occasionally, I keep my eyes peeled for the smaller miracles that happen every day. Most people call them coincidences or serendipity. I prefer to think of them as miracles.

Parking spots are one of my favorite examples of everyday miracles. I know it sounds ridiculous, but I am sure you can imagine yourself racing to an important appointment or meeting. Your mind is in overdrive. You hit traffic, and you know you will be arriving with only minutes to spare, or worse, you may even be late. You also know parking is awful in the area. You pray you find a spot.

As you get closer to your destination, you notice the area is extremely busy. Your heart sinks, preparing to drive around and waste time searching for somewhere to park. As you arrive, to your amazement you see one open spot, and it is directly in front of the door you need to enter.

Some would call this luck or coincidence. I prefer to call it an answered prayer—a miracle. That is all it takes, a simple shift in perception to notice when the universe is working with us for our highest good! You can call it what you want, but doesn't it feel so much more satisfying to believe in miracles?

When we speak our truth, we give others permission to do the same. We also become relatable and authentic. Often people hold back from saying what is truly on their heart out of fear of ridicule, sounding silly, or whatever other reason. When we are courageous enough to show up completely and speak honestly, others will follow suit. People realize they are not alone in their thoughts and feelings. It is shared humanity, and it saves lives. People know real, and they are drawn to it.

This next lesson is a personal favorite and also one our American culture tends to disagree with. We glorify being busy, but the truth is it is okay to rest. More than okay, it is a necessity. When we are putting the pieces back together after a traumatic loss, rest allows our body to reset. Rest doesn't always mean sleeping, even though sleep is an integral factor in regulating our response to stress. It could mean sitting with a cup of tea enjoying the sunset or reclining on your couch listening to your favorite music.

Often, having a hectic schedule is simply a distraction or another way of numbing out that seems more acceptable than the other myriad ways we go about living our life on autopilot rather than with intention. In Europe, many countries shut everything down from 1:00 p.m. to 4:00 p.m., specifically for this reason. It is human to need to slow down and rest. Intend to rest daily.

Learning to accept what we can't change is a skill we all need to develop. Wrapping our head and heart around a truth we simply do not want to be true for us is so damn hard. Acceptance can be the final straw that sends us into the state of being devastated. It can feel like the point of no return. Acceptance is the first step to rebuilding and moving forward. Give yourself time and know acceptance doesn't always happen in one fell swoop. It comes in many small moments.

No one heals alone. I know I spoke about this in the community section. I reiterate it here because I prided myself on doing it all alone. I learned that while this required a certain amount of strength and fortitude, it was really my fear of being disappointed, betrayed, seen as needy... the list goes on. Bottom line, my hyper-independence was not healthy. Thank goodness my community was there for me when I needed them.

Humans are tribal. When we are hurt, we are meant to be tended to. People want to care for us. They need to do something, or they also feel helpless. The lesson I learned on community, cooperation, and sacred reciprocity—the divine nature of giving and receiving—is another reason why I share my story. It is my way of being a helper in the hard times because I have been here before. I am familiar with the road, and I can show you the way.

When we heal ourselves, we heal generations before and after us. This was a belief rooted in indigenous society. Healing my trauma and grief allowed me to break cycles of addiction, violence, and abuse so my children and grandchildren did not have to be traumatized by them. It gives rise to healthier, more secure, and confident societies when we rid ourselves of patterns of thinking, being, and doing that have been passed down for centuries from one generation to another along with the shame and secrets that go along with that. We are the torchbearers for our ancestors. It has been an honor for me to do this work on myself knowing the repercussions will be felt for years to come.

Lastly, there is no final destination in healing. There is only constant evolution. Just when you think you have gotten it, you've nailed down the lesson, the universe throws you another curveball. Such is this game of life. In baseball, if you can hit the curve you're very talented because curveballs are harder to hit but have more power potential. That means they will go further faster.

The same holds true in life. If we can learn to think of these times in life as opportunities to further our growth, we evolve faster and further. What do I mean by evolution? I mean we move from reacting to circumstances to acting intentionally and in a way that honors who we truly are. It is a divine dance between our humanness and our own level of divinity.

We don't always get to choose what happens to us, but we do get to decide how these events will sculpt us. Twenty-two years later, my life is *anything* but ordinary. It is beyond all I could have imagined possible the day my life, as I knew it, ended. My children are grown, and they are successful, happy, healthy, and incredible humans. I currently have two gorgeous grandsons. I created a business where I am honored to mentor people as they walk their own journey of grief and trauma by utilizing the tools I have compiled. I am privileged to be able to share my story all over the country. Storytelling is my favorite job. Now I can add published author to my list, and I am so freakin' proud. We made it!

Carrying this pain has certainly been a privilege. I know no better way to memorialize my husband than by using his story to make someone else's journey a bit easier.

Thank you for giving me the opportunity to do just that in this book.

Acknowledgments

This book seemed as if it was the natural next step in my evolution. I scarcely anticipated the roller coaster of emotions it would invoke. The act of laying bare my life for all to see has been a venture into unparalleled vulnerability. I have learned these are the moments I live for, where humanity proves to me time and again the power of authenticity and truth are not things of the past but rather strands that make up the golden thread of connection that stitch us all together. No one survives this life alone. I could never have written this book without the love, support, and encouragement of many people.

First and foremost, I extend my heartfelt gratitude to my children. Your unwavering belief in my vision and endless patience through the countless hours spent in solitude writing has been the cornerstone of this achievement. Vincent, Tori, and Noah, you have taught me more than I will ever teach you. In the face of devastating adversity, you chose to use your loss as motivation rather than as an excuse. Your dad would be proud of the adults you have grown into. I love you with every ounce of myself. My grandsons (and future grandbabies)—you are living proof to me that life carries on and can be overwhelmingly joyful. You will forever have a guardian angel guiding and protecting you. Lauren, thank you for being their mama and for cheering me on.

To my family, for witnessing this journey in real time and helping me through. Cooking, cleaning, watching my children—I couldn't have done it without you. Mom, thank you for encouraging me and doing whatever you could to help me achieve my goals. From babysitting every Saturday so I could go to yoga teacher training to getting me a speaking engagement at your clubhouse, you have always believed in me. You and Dan have been the best grandparents to my kids.

To those who watched me in my darkest hour and did all you could to ensure I made it through—you are too many to name, but I would not be here without you. My love to Danny Poggioli. Not one single day went by without you coming over to check on me and the kids. Sundays I knew to check the back door for bagels. It is no wonder you were Jeff's best friend. The kids and I love you.

I can't forget my FDNY family. You have been there since day one. Jimmy Molinell, you carried me through the toughest time of my life, and I know I am a handful. Jimmy Lowe, to this day you have proven over and over you are a true gentleman and a true friend. You have made our family your own. The members of Tenhouse—you have supported every endeavor I could come up with in the past twenty years. After all this time, I can say we have laughed more than we have cried. You have seen every version of me and still let me hang out in the firehouse whenever I want. You guys are the best.

I owe a deep debt of gratitude to my mentor, Tiffany Carole, whose wisdom and guidance have been instrumental in shaping not only this book but also my personal growth. Your insights, feedback, and urging to get the book done have been invaluable. You helped me transform rough ideas into polished gems. You have shown me the gifts within myself.

Tina Atherall—you have given me more opportunities than I can count, but more importantly you have been the truest friend. Life wife forever.

To my oldest and dearest friends, Sylvana Carlucci and Lisa Garden. We have survived it *all*! The entire Hilltopper community, especially Christine Carroll and Annemarie Dowling-Castronovo—as much as I wish we could go back to our high school days in the 1980s, I love what we have all grown into. Having the support of such empowered women is priceless.

Kathleen Harkin, Pamela Jeffcoat, and Earl Granville—your fearlessness in sharing your stories inspired me to be fearless in sharing mine. Thank you for being an integral part of this book and also my life.

To the incredible community of friends and colleagues who provided feedback, shared their stories, and offered their shoulders to lean on—your support has been a source of strength and inspiration. Thanks for taking the time to read my rough draft, answer my texts, and urge me to continue when I wanted to throw in the towel.

I am immensely thankful to Eric Koester and the team at Manuscripts LLC who have been part of this journey: my editors, Angela Mitchell and Angela Murray, whose keen eye and creative genius have greatly enhanced the manuscript; the designers and illustrators, whose talents have brought the pages to life; and my marketing specialist Laura Vaisman-Rivera, whose passion and dedication helped to bring *Strong and Soulful* to readers around the world. A huge shout-out to Kehkashan Khalid, my revisions editor. Your expertise guided me in crafting a book that feels exactly how I dreamed it would, and your kindness talked me off many a ledge.

To those phenomenal humans who believed so deeply in me that they invested in this journey before the book was even completed—your engagement and unwavering belief in me are the true measure of this book's value. I am humbled and honored to share this part of myself with you.

Trish Arnold	Tori Olsen
Kathleen Ryan	Carol Turner
AJ Hughes	Jack Kielty
AJ Hughes.	Jeanine Mulholland
Maura Bertotti	James Lowe
Jeff Parness	Helyn Stowe
Dana Baez	Barbara MacNair.
Kathleen Fox	Jay Lovari
Lisa Keel	Mike Ray
Bonnie Owens	Kimberly Leavy
Kathryn Carrescia	Shelley Rodriguez
Trisha Franckowski	Kathy Cunningham
Tina Atherall	Diane Lubischer
Derek Zahler	Elizabeth Haag
Kim Lovett	Jacqueline Bianchi
Daniel Gallagher	Brian Kelly

Patricia OBrien
Nichole Scaraglino
Emily Bessemer.
Katherine Geary-Fitzpatrick
Karen Mackin

Margaret Hopkins.
Daniel Cavanaugh
Jedidah Tighe
Debra Buonomo
Christopher Amendola.
Donna ONeill
Joanna Schiumo
Vincent DeGennaro
Helena Arellano
Jim Harings
Nicole Shaia
Mary Gallagher
Sara Wingerath
Babette Gallagher
Sallie Lynch
Anthony Marotta
Laura Vaisman Rivera
Robert Favata
Noah Olsen
Jim Ankoviak
Jill Adkins
James Molinell
Kevin Yenowine
Jen Barber
Vincent Tranchina
Maria Jakubik

Nancy Coluccio
Maria Tassiello
Matthew Wiatrowski.
Kathleen Farraye
Annemarie
Dowling-Castronovo.
Christine Carroll
Salvatore Argano
Joseph Foley
Cody Brooks
Earl Granville
Karolyn Earley
Kelly Farmer
Laura Lavery
Maria Deligiannis
Hannah Hawley
Deborah Fiore
Melissa Roth
Jenn Zuccone
Polly Richter
Robert Hubertz
Denise Powers
Kurt Wagner
Stacy Ropp
Anna Hickson
Daniel Murphy
Lisa Inserra
Pamela Jeffcoat
Tim Miller
Noelle Gregory
Catherine Langan
Deborah Kephart

Rhonda Drapeau
Janice Smith
Kimberly Grieger
Sylvana Carlucci
Madison Jurney
Jacqueline Tobacco
John Hammershmidt
Daniella Caputo
Mary Handy

Linda Nogales
Patricia Forsman
Linda Leone
Eric Koester
Sara Bagala
Melanie Sather
Jerermy Hagerman
Donna Murtha
Jacqueline Tobacco

NOTES

Chapter 2 Grief Defined

1. *APA Dictionary of Psychology*, 2nd ed. (Washington, DC: APA, 2016), s.v. "grief," https://www.apa.org/topics/grief#:~:text=Grief%20is%20the%20anguish%20experienced,and%20apprehension%20about%20the%20future.

2. Elizabeth Kübler-Ross and David Kessler, *On Grief and Grieving: Finding the Meaning of Grief through the Five Stages of Loss* (New York, New York: Scribner Book Company, 2007), 227.

3. Kendra Hess, "America's Death-Denying Culture," *Isn't Hospice Care Just Giving Up* (blog), Brighton Hospice, March 27, 2008, https://brightonhospice.com/death-denying-culture/.

Chapter 3 What Is a Memory, What Is a Nightmare?

1. National Museum of American History, "FDNY Poster," (Online photograph, National Museum of American History, accessed March 17, 2024), https://americanhistory.si.edu/collections/nmah_1195840.

Chapter 4 The Energy of Grief

1. Robert Sheldon, "Definition: Kinetic Energy," Electronics (blog), TechTarget, December 2022, https://www.techtarget.com/whatis/definition/kinetic-energy.

2. Brittney-Nichole Connor-Savarda, "The Science Behind Emotional Energy: Exploring the Vibrations of Our Emotional World," Emotional Intelligence Magazine, April 1, 2023, https://www.ei-magazine.com/post/the-science-behind-emotional-energy-exploring-the-vibrations-of-our-emotional-world.

3. Ibid.

4. Brittney-Nichole Connor-Savarda, "The Science Behind Emotional Energy: Exploring the Vibrations of Our Emotional World," Emotional Intelligence Magazine, April 1, 2023, https://www.ei-magazine.com/post/the-science-behind-emotional-energy-exploring-the-vibrations-of-our-emotional-world.

5. Elizabeth Kübler-Ross and David Kessler, On Grief and Grieving: Finding the Meaning of Grief through the Five Stages of Loss (New York, New York: Scribner Book Company, 2007), https://grief.com/images/pdf/5%20Stages%20of%20Grief.pdf.

6. Ilene Raymond Rush, "What Are the Physical Symptoms of Grief?" Wellness (blog), Psycom, October 17, 2022, https://www.psycom.net/physical-symptoms-of-grief.

7. Bessel van der Kolk, The Body Keeps the Score: Brain, Mind, and Body in the Healing of Trauma (New York, New York: Penguin Books, 2014), 97.

8. Ibid.

9. US Department of Veterans Affairs, Military Sexual Trauma (Washington, DC: Veterans Health Administration, 2021), https://www.mentalhealth.va.gov/docs/mst_general_factsheet.pdf.

10. Joni Sweet, "Often Kept Secret, Military Sexual Trauma Leaves Lasting Scars," Mental Health News (blog), Verywell Mind, January 18, 2023, https://www.verywellmind.com/often-kept-secret-military-sexual-trauma-leaves-lasting-scars-5208647.

Chapter 5 The Clash of the Past and Present

1. Emma Suttie, "Dealing with Grief: A TCM Perspective," Philosophy (blog), Chinese Medicine Living, accessed April 2, 2024, https://www.chinesemedicineliving.com/philosophy/the-emotions/grief-the-lungs.

2. C. Spitzer et al., "Association of Airflow Limitation with Trauma Exposure and Post-Traumatic Stress Disorder," European Respiratory 37, no. 5 (May 2011): 1068–1075, DOI: 10.1183/09031936.00028010.

3. Psychiatry Advisor Contributing Writer, "Asthma Risk Significantly Increases with Posttraumatic Stress Disorder," Anxiety Disorders (blog), Psychiatry Advisor, May 9, 2019, https://www.psychiatryadvisor.com/home/topics/anxiety/ptsd-trauma-and-stressor-related/asthma-risk-significantly-increases-with-posttraumatic-stress-disorder/.

Chapter 6 Shadows and Light: Factors Influencing Grief

1. Patrick Tyrell et al., Kübler-Ross Stages of Dying and Subsequent Models, (Treasure Island, Florida: StatPearls Publishing, 2023), https://www.ncbi.nlm.nih.gov/books/NBK507885/.

2. George A. Bonanno and Kathrin Boerner, "The Stage Theory of Grief," The Journal of the American Medical Association 297, no. 24 (July 2007): 2693–4, DOI:10.1001/jama.297.24.2693-a.

3. Sidney Zisook and Katherine Shear, "Grief and Bereavement: What Psychiatrists Need to Know," World Psychiatry 8, no. 2 (June 2009): 67–74, DOI: 10.1002/j.2051-5545.2009.tb00217.

4. APA Dictionary of Psychology, 2nd ed. (Washington, DC: APA, 2016), s.v. "attachment style," https://dictionary.apa.org/attachment-style.

5. America Psychiatric Association, "APA Offers Tips for Understanding Prolonged Grief Disorder," September 22, 2021, https://www.psychiatry.org/newsroom/news-releases/apa-offers-tips-for-understanding-prolonged-grief-disorder.

6. Kristin A. Glad et al., "The Longitudinal Association Between Symptoms of Posttraumatic Stress and Complicated Grief: A Random Intercepts Cross-Lag Analysis," Psychological Trauma 14, no. 3 (April 2021): 1–7, DOI 10.1037/tra0001087.

7. Kathleen Kelly Halverson, "How Infants Grieve | A Guide for New Adoptive Parents," Uploads (blog), Mothers Choice, last modified March 6, 2018, https://www.motherschoice.org/

app/uploads/2020/10/How-Infants-Grieve-A-guide-for-New-Adoptive-Parents.pdf.

8. Kiri Walsh et al., "Spiritual Beliefs May Affect Outcome of Bereavement: Prospective Study," BMJ 324, no. 7353 (June 2002): 1551, DOI 10.1136/bmj.324.7353.1551.

9. Danielle M. Piggott and RaeAnn E. Anderson, "Religion After Rape: Changes in Faith and Hindered Acknowledgment," J Interpers Violence 38, no. 3–4 (July 2021): 3883–3905, DOI 10.1177/08862605221109913.

10. Kenneth J. Doka, "Disenfranchised Grief in Historical and Cultural Perspective," in Handbook of Bereavement Research and Practice: Advances in Theory and Intervention, ed. M. S. Stroebe, R. O. Hansson, H. Schut, and W. Stroebe, (Washington, DC: American Psychological Association, 2008), 223–240.

11. Kylie B. Rogalla, "Anticipatory Grief, Proactive Coping, Social Support, and Growth: Exploring Positive Experiences of Preparing for Loss," Omega (Westport) 81, no. 1 (May 2020): 107–29, DOI 10.1177/0030222818761461.

12. Lynne Eldridge, "What is Anticipatory Grief?" Support and Coping (blog), Verywell Health, July 15, 2023, https://www.verywellhealth.com/understanding-anticipatory-grief-and-symptoms-2248855.

13. Meg Bernhard, "What If There's No Such Thing as Closure," The New York Times Magazine, June 2023.

Chapter 8 Courage and Your Comfort Zone

1. Centers for Disease Control and Prevention, "The Drug Overdose Epidemic: Behind the Numbers," Opioids (blog), Centers for Disease Control and Prevention, August 8, 2023, https://www.cdc.gov/opioids/data/index.html.

2. National Center for Drug Abuse Statistics, "Drug Abuse Statistics," Drug Abuse Statistics, National Center for Drug Abuse Statistics, accessed January 15, 2024, https://drugabusestatistics.org/.

3. National Institute of Alcohol Abuse and Alcoholism, "Glossary," Alcohol Facts and Statistics (blog), National Institute of Alcohol Abuse and Alcoholism, accessed April 3, 2024, https://www.niaaa.nih.gov/alcohols-effects-health/alcohol-topics/alcohol-facts-and-statistics/glossary.

4. Bessel van der Kolk, The Body Keeps the Score: Brain, Mind, and Body in the Healing of Trauma (New York, New York: Penguin Books, 2014), 33.

5. Gabor Maté, When the Body Says No: The Cost of Hidden Stress (Toronto, Ontario, Canada: Vintage Canada, 2003), 3.

Chapter 9 Breaking Chains

1. Bessel van der Kolk, The Body Keeps the Score: Brain, Mind, and Body in the Healing of Trauma (New York, New York: Penguin Books, 2014).

2. Psychology Today Staff, "Trauma," Basics (blog), Psychology Today, accessed April 3, 2024, https://www.psychologytoday.com/us/basics/trauma.

3. Ibid.

4. Danielle Carr, "Tell Me Why It Hurts," Intellegencer (blog), New York Magazine, July 31, 2023, https://nymag.com/intelligencer/article/trauma-bessel-van-der-kolk-the-body-keeps-the-score-profile.html.

5. Bessel van der Kolk, The Body Keeps the Score: Brain, Mind, and Body in the Healing of Trauma (New York, New York: Penguin Books, 2014), 33.

Chapter 10 From Trauma to Transformation

1. US Department of Veteran's Affairs, "PTSD Basics," PTSD National Center for PTSD (blog), US Department of Veteran's Affairs, accessed January 15, 2024, https://www.ptsd.va.gov/understand/what/ptsd_basics.asp.

Chapter 11 G.R.A.C.E. Defined

1. Liliana Dell'Osso et al., "Post Traumatic Growth (PTG) in the Frame of Traumatic Experiences," Clin Neuropsychiatry 19, no. 6 (December 2022): 390–393, DOI: 10.36131/cnfioritieditore20220606.

2. Kiri Walsh et al., "Spiritual Beliefs May Affect Outcome of Bereavement: Prospective Study," BMJ 324, no.7353 (June 2002): 1551, DOI 10.1136/bmj.324.7353.1551.

Chapter 13 Calming the Storm

1. Robert A. Emmons and Michael E. McCullough, "Counting Blessings Versus Burdens: An Experimental Investigation of Gratitude and Subjective Well-Being in Daily Life," Journal of Personality and Social Psychology 84, no. 2 (2003): 377–389, DOI: 10.1037/0022-3514.84.2.377.

2. Peter A. Bertocci and Richard M. Millard, Personality and the Good: Psychological and Ethical Perspectives (New York, New York: McKay, 1963), 389.

3. Robert A. Emmons and Michael E. McCullough, "Counting Blessings Versus Burdens: An Experimental Investigation of Gratitude and Subjective Well-Being in Daily Life," Journal of Personality and Social Psychology 84, no.2 (2003): 377–389, DOI: 10.1037/0022-3514.84.2.377.

4. Najma Khorrami, "Gratitude and Its Impact on the Brain and Body," Gratitude (blog), Psychology Today, September 4, 2020, https://www.psychologytoday.com/us/blog/comfort-gratitude/202009/gratitude-and-its-impact-the-brain-and-body.

Chapter 17 Movement and Intention

1. UCSF Center to Advance Trauma Informed Healthcare, "How Trauma Affects Our Health," Why Trauma? (blog), UCSF Center to Advance Trauma Informed Healthcare, accessed January 15, 2024, https://cthc.ucsf.edu/why-trauma/.

2. Vincent J. Felitti, "The Relation Between Adverse Childhood Experiences and Adult Health: Turning Gold into Lead," Perm J. 6, no.1 (Winter 2002): 44–47, DOI:10.7812/TPP/02.994.

3. Vincent J. Felitti et al., "Relationship of Childhood Abuse and Household Dysfunction to Many of the Leading Causes of Death in Adults," American Journal of Preventive Medicine 14, no. 4 (May 1998): 245-258, DOI 10.1016/s0749-3797(98)00017-8.

4. Vincent J. Felitti, "The Relation Between Adverse Childhood Experiences and Adult Health: Turning Gold into Lead," Perm J. 6, no.1 (Winter 2002): 44–47. DOI:10.7812/TPP/02.994.

5. Bessel van der Kolk, The Body Keeps the Score: Brain, Mind, and Body in the Healing of Trauma (New York, New York: Penguin Books, 2014), 97.

Chapter 21 You Are the Meaning Maker

1. Macmillan Encyclopedia of Death and Dying (London, UK: Routledge, 2001), s.v. "Memorialization, Spontaneous," https://www.encyclopedia.com/social-sciences/encyclopedias-almanacs-transcripts-and-maps/memorialization-spontaneous.

2. C. Allen Haney, et al, "Spontaneous Memorialization: Violent Death and Emerging Mourning Ritual," Omega-Journal of Death and Dying 35, 2 (October 1997): 159–171, DOI 10.2190/7U8W-540L-QWX9-1VL6

3. Gun Violence Archive, "GVA -10 Year Review," Gun Violence Archive, GunViolenceArchive.org, accessed March 18, 2023, https://www.gunviolencearchive.org.

4. Robert A. Neimeyer, Meaning Reconstruction and the Experience of Loss, (Washington, DC: American Psychological Association, 2001).

Chapter 23 Only a Thought Away

1. Jenny Streit-Horn, "A Systematic Review of Research on After-Death Communication," (dissertation, University of North Texas, 2011), https://digital.library.unt.edu/ark:/67531/metadc84284/m1/1/.

2. Jenn, "After Death Communications: How to Encourage Signs from Loved Ones in Spirit," The Search for Life After Death (blog), June 2, 2016, https://thesearchforlifeafterdeath.com/2016/05/07/after-death-communications-why-it-happens-why-it-doesnt-and-how-to-encourage-signs-from-loved-ones-in-spirit/.

Made in the USA
Middletown, DE
06 September 2024